DISSERTATION
—AND—
RESEARCH
SUCCESS

DISSERTATION
— AND —
RESEARCH
SUCCESS

HANDS-ON COACHING FOR DOCTORAL SUCCESS BEFORE, DURING, AND AFTER YOUR DISSERTATION

ROBIN BUCKLEY, PHD AND TIMOTHY DELICATH, PHD

Library of Congress Control Number:		2012923976
ISBN:	Hardcover	978-1-4797-6428-0
	Softcover	978-1-4797-6427-3
	Ebook	978-1-4797-6429-7

This book was printed in the United States of America.

Rev. Date: 02/15/2013

To order additional copies of this book, contact:
Xlibris Corporation
1-888-795-4274
www.Xlibris.com
Orders@Xlibris.com
105226

CONTENTS

Dedication

To our spouses, Lisa and Tom,
whose support and love make everything possible . . .

FOREWORD

It would be easier to quit. Completing a doctoral program is not easy, and trying to complete a dissertation at the end of your program when the last of your energy and motivation is hanging by a string, can seem insurmountable. So, yes, it would be easier to quit. There are even individuals out in the world who proudly use the acronym "ABD" (all-but-dissertation) as their terminal "degree" on resumes, business cards and such. But in all honesty, I can tell you what ABD really stands for—quitting. You've invested too much time, energy and money into your doctoral experience to give up. With that being said, this is not an easy journey. Finding resources and support to help you navigate through your doctoral program in the most efficient and painless way is an absolute.

I met Robin when we were in graduate school together. By the end of the first week in our traditional program, we had approximately 1200 pages of reading to accomplish by the following week's classes. (It was amazing a few of us did not drop out of the program right then.) Robin managed to come up with a strategy, and organized our group of 25 strangers to work together to complete the readings. As our friendship grew, I learned that Robin was the type of person who wanted to do everything to the best of her ability, but who realized that sometimes you need to rely on others in order to get the "to do" list completed. Her integration of helping others through the learning process continued to develop in graduate school, and it did not surprise me when she became an adjunct professor for a private college in her second year of our program. This seemed like a natural fit for her and a place for her to continue to help others enhance their own learning experiences. Over the years, I have watched Robin broaden her approach to encompass doctoral education, finding ways to make the doctoral experience as enjoyable, effectual and straightforward as possible.

Through Robin, I met Tim. When you meet both of them, it is obvious why they are not only good friends, but more importantly, why their collaboration has such a powerful impact on the doctoral students they work with. Tim's whole focus is to help his students, in any way possible. I have witnessed him as a cheerleader, an advocate, and an unconditional supporter for his students. I often call Tim a "research Sherpa" because he guides and directs students to get to their research and educational goals while taking the unnecessary weight of the doctoral degree off their shoulders. Without feelings of confusion, being overwhelmed, or lost, Tim's students focus on true learning and, as a result, successfully complete their degrees. He spends hours puzzling over students' issues to determine the best ways to help them learn what they need to in order to accomplish objectives and keep moving toward their goals.

You can imagine how the blend of these two personalities benefits students. When Robin and Tim approached me to read their book, and write a forward, I was initially a little surprised that they had written what I called a "dissertation textbook". There are plenty of dissertation "how to" books out there, and knowing this pair, a dry, stand-offish textbook did not match who I know them to be. The first chapter set the tone for the whole book, however, and I quickly realized what makes their book different from all the others—I heard their voices in the writing. In other words, it was written as if the authors were talking directly to the reader, rather than sitting behind some desk or standing behind a classroom lectern. The authors in this workbook created easy to read chapters, blending in experience, observations and support among the dissertation-related information. They used activities to enhance the learning, allowing their readers to practice their skills right within the workbook text. Reading *Dissertation and Research Success*, I imagined being back in my own graduate program with a book like this. Instead of the weighty and cumbersome language inherent to many graduate textbooks, here was a book written for students, speaking to them, in a personal, meaningful way.

As I said at the beginning of this forward, finding resources to make your doctoral process as painless as possible is an absolute. Completing the degree you started is also an absolute. Robin and Tim have pulled together faculty who are experts in their fields, and who have years of experience working with doctoral students. You get the advantage of not only their knowledge, but their shared desire to help doctoral students succeed. I can honestly say I wish a resource such as this workbook had been available when I was in graduate school, and I plan to keep it as my own resource for work with graduate students and research in my organization.

Tom Grebouski, Ph.D.
Chief of Psychology
Monarch School of New England

ACKNOWLEDGEMENTS

This first edition of *Dissertation and Research Success: Hands-on coaching approach before, during, and after your dissertation* is the product of collaborative efforts from many individuals who share one common goal—to help doctoral students achieve their dreams. First and foremost, we would like to thank our colleagues who made significant contributions to the content of the book, namely Suzanne Beier, Barbara Shambaugh, Kelley Conrad, Linda de Charon and Ron Hutkin. Their patience as we developed the idea of this "workbook", and more importantly, the knowledge they offer in their respective chapters truly reflects their dedication to doctoral learning. They did not write these chapters for status or financial gain. They agreed to be part of this project because of their innate desire to make the dissertation process manageable for doctoral candidates.

In particular, we want to thank Tiffany Tibbs for offering both her creative and editorial expertise in the development of this workbook, as well as within her chapters. Without her enthusiasm and involvement in the "deadline" stages, this would have been a much more arduous process. She proved that writing, editing, and talking about research can actually be fun.

We also thank Tom Grebouski for writing the Foreword. Tom's background mentoring doctoral students, combined with his experience in "doing what [you guys] teach", offered us an objective perspective on our work. We appreciate his candor, support and friendship through this process.

When setting out to write a book, the logistics of publishing can be a daunting task and the process is not for the faint-hearted. Because of this, we are extremely grateful for the direction and encouragement of the staff at Xlibris. Offering doctoral students a "non-textbook" style dissertation guide was a perfect match for self-publishing, one that was recognized by the staff at Xlibris who provided an avenue to finally made our ideas into reality.

Throughout our own careers, we have been blessed to have mentors, colleagues and students who have inspired us to find the best methods to take the mystery out of dissertation development. Their topical knowledge, instructional strategies and passion for learning were the motivation for the creation of this book.

Finally, we want to offer our deepest gratitude to our families: Tom, Jordan, Madison, Justin, Lisa, Viki, Tad and Cassie. They have been incredibly patient, waiting for us to stop talking about the book and "get it done". Without their unconditional belief in us, and their support, this book would have likely stayed a thought.

EDITORS

Robin Buckley earned her Ph.D. in Clinical and School Psychology. She has 15 years of experience working in clinical and public school settings, as well as within higher education administration and instruction. She currently facilitates online doctoral courses and chairs doctoral dissertations in the areas of Education, Business and Health Administration. Dr. Buckley also conducts executive coaching for business leaders in corporate and non-profit organizations. Her coaching practice also includes working with doctoral students in traditional and online programs, focusing on dissertation coaching and advising.

Timothy A. Delicath earned his Ph.D. degree in Higher Education Administration with a Minor in Research and Statistics from Saint Louis University. He has over 30 years of experience in secondary and post-secondary education as an educator and administrator. His roles include teacher, professor, director of institutional research, director of academic affairs, and other administrative positions. Tim has facilitated online doctoral level courses for the past 12 years. He has also served as dissertation chair and committee member for both quantitative and qualitative studies. He has done consulting work in the areas of business process development, research study design and implementation, data-driven decision making, institutional research, strategic planning, and assessment and evaluation for multiple organizations.

CONTRIBUTORS

Kelley A. Conrad earned his Ph.D. in Industrial Organizational Psychology. He was a business psychologist with the firm of Humber, Mundie, and McClary in Milwaukee, WI for 25 years. For ten years he was self-employed as a business consultant and manager of a public service non-profit internet service provider. He has been a research and academic faculty member for doctoral studies for an online university where he was recently recognized as a faculty of the year. He has served as a doctoral chair and as a committee member for a number of successful doctoral students. Dr. Conrad has co-authored two books, presented and authored a number of professional papers. He is a fellow of the Wisconsin Psychological Association and the American Psychological Society.

Linda de Charon, Ph.D. has earned degrees in engineering, systems technology management, and leadership decision sciences. She supported federal government satellite and space shuttle programs as an engineer and supported intelligence programs as a strategic planner for nearly 30 years. Linda has been an online doctoral studies instructor since 2004 and has also been facilitating traditional doctoral courses and reviewing doctoral proposals and dissertations since 2007. She is currently a lead faculty area chair for doctoral research and dissertations.

Ron Hutkin earned his Ph.D. degree in higher Education Administration and Research from Southern Illinois University. He has over 33 years of experience in public and private Community College/Technical Institute administration in positions from Dean to President. He has also served as Higher Learning Commission C/E and directed both state and federally funded research projects. For the past 8 years he has been facilitating doctoral courses online and on ground as well as serving as a dissertation chair and committee member for both quantitative and qualitative studies.

Barbara F. Shambaugh, RN, Ed.D. is a nurse and researcher with a primary interest in the doctoral student and the dissertation process. She has a particular interest in nursing theory and theory development. As a doctoral faculty member, she supports student work in the classroom as well as the dissertation. Her clinical work included a long interest in transplantation and dialysis. She has worked extensively with theoretical nursing with Dr. Betty Neuman and her Systems Model for nursing education, practice and research.

Tiffany L. Tibbs earned her Ph.D. in Clinical Psychology, with a specialization in Health Psychology. She has been a research faculty member at a traditional university medical school and has served as a faculty member for doctoral studies at an online university. She has been actively involved in the academic research setting as a behavioral scientist on a number of nationally-funded research studies. She has extensive experience reviewing doctoral dissertation proposals for quality methods, and mentoring postdoctoral fellows, graduate students, undergraduates, and research staff.

Susanne Beier, Ph.D. is a Licensed Professional Counselor (LPC) in Pennsylvania and New Jersey and also a Diplomate-Disability Analyst and Diplomate Forensic Counselor. In addition she is a Nationally Certified Counselor (NCC) and Master Career Counselor (MCC). Dr. Beier founded Susanne Parente Associates, a counseling firm consulting to educational and corporate clients (Fortune 500 companies). She has taught for both traditional and online programs at the undergraduate, graduate and doctorate level for 10 years. She is also a Doctoral Dissertation Chair and sits on several dissertation committees. She was featured in NEW WOMAN, Working Woman, SELF and Cosmopolitan magazines for her work with corporate relocation clients.

CHAPTER 1

Surviving Your Dissertation

Susanne Beier, PhD; Robin Buckley, PhD; and Barbara F. Shambaugh, EdD

You're finally here—ready to start or in the process of writing your doctoral dissertation. You've successfully finished many years of coursework, which may have included residencies, practicums, or internships. (By the way, congratulations on this! This is a huge accomplishment—you should be proud!)

Now you have this one last thing to complete, right? The dissertation. Of course, this one last thing feels like it is the size of an elephant! Most doctoral students experience challenges when it comes to their dissertation. These challenges tend to fall into two categories: research and personal. Believe it or not, the research challenges are actually the easier ones to address. These may include things such as scholarly writing, knowing methodology and design, creating a comprehensive literature review, collecting data, and knowing the information to put in each chapter of your dissertation. Why do I say these are easier to manage? Because all these can be taught or tutored with the help of guides, such as the one in your hands right now, or by hiring consultants to help you develop the necessary skills to complete your dissertation.

The other category is a bit more difficult to control: personal. In this category is you: your motivation and energy, time management, family and friends, other life responsibilities, and confidence. Finding a way to get all of these under control and use them in an efficient and productive way is truly half the battle of getting your dissertation done.

So How Is This Book Going to Help You?

You obviously know there are many "how to write a dissertation" books on the market. What makes this one different? First, the topics in this book are going to address both your needs as a person and your needs as a doctoral student. Second, when we were completing our own dissertations, we didn't want to read another textbook. What we wanted was to have a personal connection with experienced faculty who could explain details of the dissertation in an easy-to-understand way so we didn't have to bother our chairs or committee members every time we had a question. We also wanted some hands-on opportunities to help us understand topics related to the dissertation development, so we learned the information in a multimodal process.

This book was developed based upon these ideas. Each chapter is written by a doctoral faculty member with experience in helping students complete their dissertations. Each chapter is written as if the author is sitting across you, talking to you personally. You'll also find activities and worksheets throughout the chapters and in the appendices to help you develop a clearer understanding of the dissertation development process—from topic generation, to committee selection, to oral defense.

Before we can dive into the parts of the dissertation, we need to establish your plan . . .

Surviving Your Dissertation

At the beginning of the dissertation process, most doctoral students wonder how they will accomplish this huge undertaking. My response is a question: "How do you eat an elephant?" The answer? "One . . . bite . . . at . . . a . . . time!" The same is true of your dissertation. You won't be able to get it all done at once, and worrying about it all is a waste of energy. While this is a wonderful analogy, let's be honest. It is hard not to feel overwhelmed by your dissertation. How do you realistically get it all done? How do you find time for all the other parts of your life? How do you keep your sanity while doing all that? Before you dive into the reading, researching, and writing of your dissertation, let's talk about something even more important: *how to survive your dissertation.*

The Dissertation Is Not Your Life

We're going to say something you likely have not heard often, if at all: your dissertation is not your life. While it is a big part of your life, you have many other parts of your life, which need to be factored in to this big project plan. Although the doctoral program is a significant part of your life, it is not your life. When you finish your degree, your job, family, and friends will still be there. You can't neglect them (or your own needs) or put them on hold until you finish. Finding ways to integrate them into the process, and vice versa, is a challenging aspect of your education.

With the workload of any doctoral program, we know it is easy to just put your head down and plow, full steam, straight ahead. Somehow, however, we still need to take time—even if it's just five to ten minutes per day—to reflect, relax, take a deeeeep breath, or whatever we find personally helpful. To lose touch with ourselves, or our support system (family, friends), is a mistake that many doctoral students make at some point in their educational process. Unfortunately, too many doctoral students sacrifice their personal lives for their education, only to end up with only their degree (having lost their family, friends, jobs, health, or aspects of each). Always keep in mind the idea of homeostasis, or balance, in your life. Each important part must fit in, must be juggled, in order to make it all worthwhile when you're done.

Juggling All the Balls

There are eight facets of your life that you must address every day in order to have a balance within your life.

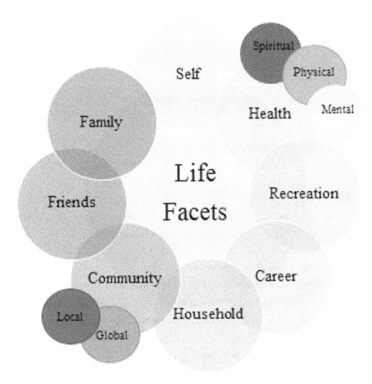

This juggling act is no simple feat, and when you insert something like your dissertation into the mix, it's like adding a bowling ball among the eight regular balls! Before we discuss how to maintain balance in all areas of your life, let me create a list of terms just like in chapter 1 of your dissertation to explain the life facets:

Self: personal development, intellectual, growth, and practical living

Health: your spiritual health (faith, spiritual growth, strengthening of your beliefs), physical health (exercise, diet, overall well-being), and mental health (relaxation, stress management)

Recreation: fun, leisure activities, and vacation planning

Family: your relationship with your spouse, children, parents, or other relatives

Friends: your circle of friends and enriching existing relationships

Community: commitment to serving others through your time, talent, and dedication on local and global levels

Career: skills development, networking, and future ambitions

Household: finances, household improvements, security, and general maintenance

Are you starting to feel that overwhelming tightness in your chest again as you look over this list and think, "Where the heck am I going to find time to do all that *and* finish my dissertation?" First, consider this: you are likely doing things in each category already, so you don't have to start all new things in order to find this balance. Second, we're going to use the following activity to allow you the opportunity to reassure yourself that you are addressing all facets of your life as well as see what areas need a little extra from you. On the next four pages, there are charts for each facet of your life. We usually recommend to dissertation coaching clients that they identify one goal that they can do daily, one goal weekly, and one goal monthly and/or yearly for each facet. Be sure to insert activities that you may already be doing and then use the charts to ensure you *keep doing these activities*. You also might find that some activities can fit in more than one chart. For example, in one of the author's personal goal-setting charts, she has "20 minutes of pure *fun* with kids" as a daily goal in both her Recreation chart and her Family chart. If she decides that fun will be doing yoga with kids, that goal can then also go in to either the daily or the weekly goal for Health as well. Don't forget in your Self chart to include your dissertation work; this is certainly an activity that is part of your personal and intellectual development!

Self

List three goals relating to development, intellectual, growth, and practical living.

Practical Goals
Daily:
Weekly:
Monthly/yearly:

Health

List three goals relating to your spiritual health (faith, spiritual growth, strengthening of your beliefs), physical health (exercise, diet, overall well-being), and mental health (relaxation, stress management).

Practical Goals
Daily:
Weekly:
Monthly/yearly:

Recreation

List three goals relating to relaxation, leisure activities, and vacation planning.

Practical Goals
Daily:
Weekly:
Monthly/yearly:

My Family

List three goals relating to your relationship with your spouse, children, parents, or other relatives.

Practical Goals
Daily:
Weekly:
Monthly/yearly:

My Friends

List three goals relating to maintaining your circle of friends, and enriching existing relationships.

Practical Goals
Daily:
Weekly:
Monthly/yearly:

My Community

List three goals relating to your commitment to serving others through your time, talent and dedication on local and global levels.

Practical Goals
Daily:
Weekly:
Monthly/yearly:

My Career

List three goals relating to skills development, networking, and future ambitions.

Practical Goals
Daily:
Weekly:
Monthly/yearly:

My Household

List three goals relating to finances, household improvements, security, and general maintenance.

Practical Goals
Daily:
Weekly:
Monthly/yearly:

Definition of Recreation

Since few doctoral students regularly use this word in their vocabularies, let's be sure you know what it means. Recreation = fun—fun for the sake of having fun and relaxing. Seems like a foreign word to you right now, huh? Fun is a necessary part of surviving your dissertation and maintaining your optimal level of functioning. It reduces stress, increases creativity, provides clarity of thought, and enhances both physical and mental health. Unfortunately, most adults have to work hard to find ways to have fun and reduce stress (which is sometimes stress-inducing in itself). If you're in this category, consider watching some of the kids in your life or reflecting back to your own childhood. Children have the innate ability to be in the moment and find fun in simple activities.

Here is your challenge: Think of some things that used to bring you real pleasure when you were younger. Whether it was running or walking *just to run or walk* (rather than to exercise), reading the comics and really enjoying them, rolling in the grass (okay, your neighbors might wonder about you if you don't have kids to justify your behavior), swinging on a swing, stargazing, whatever. That of course isn't the challenge. The challenge to you is *to do it* more than once. You'll need to come up with many options to relieve stress through the dissertation process, and sometimes you'll need to be creative and spontaneous. Take this as an opportunity to explore some options, before the stress of your dissertation depletes your health.

Kids are great role models for us adults in another area as well—using creativity when we are critically analyzing situations. Most adults have experienced this lack of creativity, when they can't see all the options or solutions to a situation, particularly when they are under high levels of stress. Each of us had this creative ability when we were children. (Remember the fun you had with paper towel roles, cardboard boxes, and Tupperware?) But somewhere in our development, our creativity was stifled in lieu of pragmatism. Recapturing that creativity is a valuable strategy to enhance our critical thinking, a valuable tool in dissertation development.

The Japanese culture supports the development of creativity for this reason. Creativity is encouraged in Japanese elementary schools in the subjects of math and science but discouraged in discussions of social issues related to the rigid status quo. At the elementary school level, a child-centered, "whole child approach to education is dominant" (Benjamin & James, 1998, as cited in Edwards, 2004, p. 22). In the first grade, Japanese children are given four times more playtime at school than American children in order to help develop their creativity in a supportive, caring environment virtually void of competition (a situation that changes completely

> *Recapturing that creativity is a valuable strategy to enhance our critical thinking, a valuable tool in dissertation development.*

once they reach high school and creativity is stifled). Edwards states, "Impressive amounts of creativity, free play, spontaneity, learner autonomy, a willingness to make mistakes and learn from them, and intrinsic motivation are already at the heart of the current Japanese educational system, forming the very foundation of the national curriculum in the first, most formative years of schooling" (2004, p. 23). The success of young Japanese students on international math and science tests may be attributed in part to the importance placed on creativity and free play in elementary school. Your success as a doctoral student can be enhanced when you have a balanced life that includes time for recreation.

Using Your Strengths

Now that you've outlined how you will maintain balance in all eight facets of your life throughout the dissertation process, we need to discuss your biggest obstacle—you! Throughout this process, there will likely be times when you feel like you just can't finish. This might manifest itself as depression or anger and frustration or physical exhaustion. In these cases, the following exercise will be valuable.

Identify a very difficult event in your life, a situation or time you didn't think you'd be able to get through but in which you did experience success. Write it down on the following lines.

_____
_____
_____
_____
_____

What thoughts went through your mind as you began this situation, and you realized how difficult it was going to be?

_____
_____
_____
_____
_____

What physical feelings did you experience in your body as the situation became more difficult?

_____
_____
_____
_____

How did you feel in those moments when it felt like things were not going to work out as you wanted? What thoughts crossed your mind?

_____

_____

_____

_____

_____

The situation you identified was one that was incredibly hard, but one in which you successfully survived. What personal characteristics made that situation successful? What internal attributes helped you keep moving forward even when things were difficult? List them here.

_____

_____

_____

_____

_____

What positive thoughts helped you persevere and succeed in that situation?

_____

_____

_____

_____

_____

What behaviors helped you in that situation?

_____

_____

_____

_____

_____

How did you feel about yourself when you succeeded?

_____

_____

_____

_____

_____

Now consider your doctoral program. This, too, will be one of the hardest things you've undertaken in your life. In those moments when you feel like quitting, when you feel like you are completely overwhelmed with writing your dissertation, look back at the list of qualities that helped you through equally, or more, challenging situations. If those qualities were what made you survive in the past, these are inherent parts of your personality and, therefore, still a part of you. All you have to do is tap into them again in order to keep moving forward to tackle your dissertation and accomplish your goal of becoming a Doctor.

> *"If you're training for a triathlon, you don't want to talk to the guy watching you train. You want to talk to the guy training right alongside of you, feeling the same sweat and pains."*

Working With a Peer Who Is in the Trenches

No one knows what it is like for you right at the moment. Your family and friends are sympathetic, but none of them have likely ever been in a doctoral program. Even if they have, they haven't been in yours, right at this moment, dealing with your topic, and your committee. Yours is a very unique experience. The only people who could come close to truly knowing what it is like to be in your shoes are your cohort peers, or at least members of your program. They know what it is like to be in the trenches with you.

One way to help you imagine your task ahead is to use an analogy. One of the best analogies to the dissertation is Dorothy's journey down the yellow brick road in *The Wizard of Oz*. Why? All of Dorothy's problems derive from her fears and confusion, but ultimately her courage, problem solving, and support helped her every step of the way. Dorothy came into a world she did not understand, and fought her way through until she understood that she was in charge of herself.

The early journey involved finding her team—the Scarecrow, the Tin Man, and the Cowardly Lion. She could not

Develop a support team who are all in the same situation. Having a ready support team to critique your writing and your content is critical to your success. Asking for feedback is your lifeline to success. And, it is just as important to provide feedback to your support team as well. Building your own team, provides you with the possibility of support, critique, valuable feedback from your team and providing feedback as well.

* Find three or four colleagues involved in the dissertation process.

* Distribute contact information (e-mails, cell numbers, Skype addresses) and consider creating a forum to meet (Facebook group, online blog, Google Office).

*Agree to support each team member by providing feedback to each other.

* Share information on research, findings in the literature and reviews of related dissertations.

have done this alone. The support she received was exactly what she needed. She felt a level of danger and the support of her colleagues sustained her moving forward each step of the journey. You can find your team from classes, work groups, workshops, and by word of mouth. It might take a bit of time, but the rewards are many and varied. To have a dialogue that helps you focus on your problem, to have help with tightening up your writing, and to have someone tell you to get back with it stay with it are all examples of what a peer support group can be for you.

Hadjioannou, Shelton, Fu, and Dhanarattigannon (2007) shared their experiences as doctoral students and how helpful it was they had each other to support and rely on when things became frustrating. They found that by being supportive peers, two effects were created. First, they were able to reduce the stress of the doctoral experience for each other. Second, the peer support helped them develop from being a doctoral learner to becoming an academic scholar. They describe interacting with other doctoral students as a powerful means of socialization that reduced a feeling they were are all alone in their doctoral journey. By experiencing shared common goals, dreams and concerns with their peers, they felt a sense of belonging and security that supported them through periods of doubt and insecurity. Does all this sound familiar? This peer support or network becomes particularly important when it comes to the many rewrites typical in the dissertation writing process.

You need to have a doctoral peer support group. The number of peers is not as important as the connection and support you give each other. It can be as little as one peer or as many as a whole group, but ultimately those individuals will understand your experience because it is their experience. When you have questions, they'll likely have answers or will give you sources to find your answers. When you need an objective read of your draft, they will provide you a safe place prior to submitting it to your committee. When you just need to vent, they'll understand far better than your very patient loved ones. And when you feel like quitting, they will be the ones to listen, empathize, and then pull you back up.

Time Management

We'd love to tell you that only incredibly intelligent individuals end up earning their doctoral degrees. While being smart certainly helps, this is truly not the defining characteristic that results in having *Dr.* in front of your name. What is it then? The majority of individuals who have earned their doctorates would agree that the defining characteristic between doctors and ABDs (all but dissertation) is stubbornness. Whether you call it *tenacity, diligence,* or *determination,* it simply comes down to the fact that these graduating doctoral candidates did . . . not . . . give . . . up. Part of their decision to successfully write their dissertations and, ultimately, graduate involved creating a plan how to manage their dissertation work time. As a good friend, Dr. Tom Patrizio, has said, "A dissertation is an exercise in time-on-task." To avoid wasting your time in a lengthy discussion about dissertation writing strategies, let's create an easy checklist for you to use when planning your time on task.

> *"A dissertation is an exercise in time-on-task."*

Steps to Create Your Dissertation Writing Plan

_____ 1. Create a consistent workplace in which to do your research, reading, and writing. Ideally this is a place where you can leave your notes, articles, and other materials and they will not get disturbed. This space should become your academic bubble where you can focus on your dissertation.

_____ 2. Make a schedule. Decide on what days and at what time each day you will actively work on your dissertation. My recommendation to students is to plan at least thirty minutes every day for dissertation work. By devoting time each day to your dissertation, you create a habit. On days you might choose not to work on it, there should be a strange feeling of *something I should be doing* and this alone may motivate you to go work on your dissertation. Once you decide on your schedule, *write it down*. In fact, utilize that Type A personality you have and write it down in multiple locations—on your cell phone's calendar, on a paper calendar in your work area, anywhere that will remind or nag you to stick to your schedule.

_____ 3. Make a completion plan timeline. This is different from your daily schedule. Your timeline details your milestones in the dissertation process (i.e., completed chapter 1, submission to chair and committee for review, IRB submission, etc.), culminating with your oral defense date. The easiest way to create this timeline is to start with the oral defense and work backward. When you do this, you can quickly see whether your chosen date is realistic or whether you need to change your work schedule to meet that selected deadline. Be sure to build in "cushions" within the timeline for any unforeseen delays in getting drafts out or getting reviews back. It is easier to gain time on your timeline than have to build extra time in. Your timeline is also a concrete tool to keep you to your schedule. Say, for example, you decide to take a day off from your dissertation work. Go to your timeline and add one day on to the end; in other words, move your oral defense date up by one day. Do this each time you take a day off from your dissertation writing. You will see quickly how time now affects time later.

Dissertation and Research Success   31

_____ 4. Make a list of all the things you need to accomplish to finish your dissertation. The list should consider every single thing you'll need to do to get your dissertation through your oral defense. Once you make this list, organize it according to time and energy level needed to complete each one. You might choose to highlight the easy tasks in green, moderate tasks in yellow and high level tasks in red. Or you could create three separate lists, organized by these three categories. Once you do this, you now have options for how to productively use your time. On days when you have an extra fifteen minutes to work on your dissertation, you might pick something off your easy list to get done. On a day when you find yourself with lots of energy and time, you can choose something off your *high level* list. In this way, you will consistently use your time in a productive manner. Until your dissertation passes the oral defense, there is never a moment when you couldn't be doing something to get closer to the finish line.

_____ 5. Purchase a large wall calendar for your workspace. Using the information from your timeline and the overall list of things you need to do, set monthly and weekly goals. Determine a goal that you want to have accomplished by the end of one month. Write this goal in the last day of that month. Now break this goal into four objectives, with the idea that if you complete each objective, the goal will be accomplished. Write one objective at the end of each week of that month. Now look at each weekly objective; break the objective down to daily action items. You should have between one and three action items written on each day of the week. These should be specific, measurable, and manageable tasks that can be done in the time allotted for your daily dissertation work. As you complete each action item, and then each objective, cross them off on your calendar. While this reinforces your steady progress, it will also be helpful at the end of the month. Your action item on the last day of the month must be to evaluate your progress during that month. You may choose to use the following process in your evaluation.

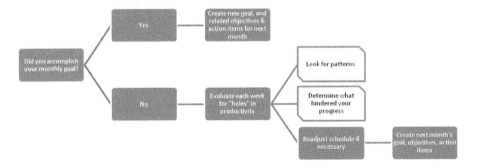

So often, doctoral students force themselves to stick to the schedule even when the schedule is not working for them because they don't take the time to assess the validity of their tool. By incorporating an evaluation at the end of each month, you will avoid the tendency to keep repeating a schedule or process that is not effective.

_____ 6. At the end of each work session, leave yourself a note regarding where you were in the writing process so you don't have to spend fifteen minutes in your next session trying to figure out where you left off and what you were focusing on last time. If you can leave a session by leaving questions for yourself to consider in the next work session, or things to do the next time you sit down, you'll also waste less time trying to get started.

Don't Put Off Living

"I'm going to treat myself to a full spa day."
"I'm going to take my family on a cruise."
"I'm going to reconnect with my friends."
"I'm going to have a big party to celebrate."

These are just some of the rewards we've heard doctoral students planning for when they are finally done with their dissertation and all requirements of their doctoral programs. It is nice to daydream or even start planning for a big celebration once you are have eaten that whole elephant, and you certainly deserve it. But you also need to enjoy life and reward yourself for the small accomplishments along the way. We've already discussed the importance of enjoying all facets of your life earlier in this chapter, and you created charts to help remember and devote time to those eight facets. Some activities on those charts may be rewards for you, and there may be other things that don't fit on those charts but that you would enjoy as a reward.

Right next to your calendar, timeline, and to do lists, create a Rewards list. Like your to-do list, you might organize it according to small rewards, moderate rewards, and big rewards. (These may even correspond to your easy, moderate, and high-level activities.) They may be unique, one-time types of activities, or they may be smaller activities that you can use repeatedly to celebrate accomplishments on your dissertation. The challenge with a rewards list is to only allow yourself a reward once you have fully and successfully completed a task. Don't cheat by giving yourself a reward before you have finished!

The importance of living life even during the doctoral process really impacted a colleague of ours. In graduate school, our colleague had a close friend named Maria. In their first class of the doctoral program, Maria introduced herself by stating the date she was going to have her oral defense—four years in the future! Our colleague stated throughout their program, Maria diligently worked to support herself through school and devoted herself to her studies. When the rest of the students would take time to relax or de-stress from their rigorous academic schedule, Maria would politely turn them down to work so she could work or study. She rarely went home to visit her family. According to our colleague, Maria often said, "I'll have fun when I'm done." Maria didn't defend on the date she selected . . . she defended two days earlier! She had a 4.0 average in her graduate classes, and passed her oral defense with no revisions required. At the end of her defense, our colleague asked Maria how she was finally going to celebrate. Maria pulled a plane ticket from her jacket pocket, and excitedly shared she was going on a month-long trip to Australia—her lifelong dream.

Maria's plane was scheduled to leave one week after her defense. The day following her defense, Maria's car was struck by a drunk driver and she died.

> *Don't put off living.*

That story leaves us with a powerful lesson that sacrificing living, any and all aspects of it, is not worth it.

Sabotage Within the Dissertation Process

Herr (1979) posited that educational success and work success are frequently matters of "personal adjustment and are frequently matters of interpersonal skill such as clarifying one's self-identity" (p. 26). How does this relate to doctoral studies? It means that doctoral students who have a good sense of self, will persist and can find meaning in what they are learning or what they want to accomplish, and will successfully complete their dissertation. Does that mean if one has not achieved a good sense of self-identity, that student is doomed to fail and cannot complete doctoral studies? No, not at all; it just means that person needs to identify what is holding him or her back, and what is sabotaging his or her success. Let me introduce you to three saboteurs to doctoral success: fear of failure, fear of success, and the silent saboteur.

Fear of Failure

This saboteur manifests itself as a deep feeling that you can't do whatever goal you have set for yourself. Maybe you perceive others as doubting you'll be able to accomplish this goal. You worry you'll make a fool of yourself, or that people will see you as a failure. You question whether it is worth the effort to even try since you may not be able to finish.

Fear of Success

Fear of success is the perception that you do not deserve the success you are about to achieve. Why would someone be afraid of that? It relates to fear of change. Life may be different once you become a doctor. Your relationships may change. You may fear that accomplishing your goal may jeopardize the life you have now. Some fears of success are easy to let go because they are unrealistic and will probably never happen. For example, one unrealistic fear of doctoral student may be the fear they will be working at a fast-food restaurant with a doctoral degree, or become a homeless person and lose it all. Other fears of success are real. For example, when you change, the relationships around you change. Some friends will stay with you until the end. Others who are steeped in jealousy or afraid you are going to outgrow them may belittle you as you are moving forward.

- Revisit the event you described in the Using Your Strengths activity. Remind yourself that you have overcome this, and many, challenging situations in your life.
- Take five minutes of quiet meditation or thought to reflect on the academic accomplishments you've already made in your life.
- Consider your loved ones and friends. The reality is that they believe in you, even when you might not.

The Silent Saboteurs

Finally, you may experience silent saboteurs in your doctoral program. These may be both external voices and internal voices. External silent saboteurs are typically the group of people you expect the most support and understanding from: your family and friends. While one aspect of their relationship with you is supportive, there is also the other side, which misses having your full attention. They may experience a competitive reaction to your dissertation work. You might begin to hear comments such as, "You are never around," or "You're always working on your dissertation." The result is feeling guilty and not focusing on writing the dissertation as is necessary to succeed.

- Create a fear list. Make a two-column chart. One column's heading is UNREALISTIC and   the other is REALISTIC. Whenever you have a fear regarding your future success, analyze to determine which column it belongs in. Write it down.
- For any fears in the REALISTIC column, write one to three strategies that you can do to mitigate those fears. For example, if you are fearful of losing a friendship, determine an action you could do to foster the friendship during your dissertation process. You might also consider talking to anyone related to a realistic fear to share your worries. You may be pleasantly surprised by person's reaction!

There is also your internal silent saboteur, described by Fritsch (2002) as your self-saboteur. This is the part of you that may believe you are undeserving of joy and success, that you are an imposter who does not deserve to have succeeded as far as you have. The students who have shared these feelings with us are nervous, frightened, and feel (as they have said) they "don't belong in this program," or "I don't think I'm smart enough to do this." The focus is not on what they have achieved, but instead on what they feel they cannot achieve. Many of their thoughts derive back to the fear of failure and fear of success, which was discussed earlier.

- Plan a family or friend meeting. Share your plans, intentions, and needs. Ask what you can do for each member of your family. Identify what will be required. Let the family know that there will be time-outs for family time.
- Make sure you keep your promise.

Taking a Break

There are times when your personal life must take priority over your academics. Now, we are not advocating taking breaks in your program; if you can avoid doing this, you're less likely to quit as it is human nature to procrastinate getting back to something once we walk away from it. However, you know your own situation. If there is a situation in your personal life that is taking an excessive amount of energy or creating excessive stress, you must put aside any perfectionistic tendencies most doctoral students have, and acknowledge that maybe you can't do it all right at the moment. Situations don't always include severe emergencies like family illness or death. Sometimes, we just need a mental break. Trust me, if you're just plowing ahead and functioning on low fuel, you really aren't getting all you should be out of your program. You know whether you're just a little overtaxed this week or if it really is a pervasive feeling that needs to be addressed. If you make the choice to put your doctoral program on hold, you must set a plan *in writing* on when to get back on track in the program. This is paramount to ensuring that you will complete your degree. Consider this like a contract with yourself—allowing you time to deal with the personal situation but creating a deadline and plan for when you will get back into your program or dissertation writing.

- Focus on the concrete facts of what you have achieved rather than the possibility of what may happen.
- Redo the activity from Using Your Strengths but identify a different scenario.
- Take five minutes of quiet meditation or thought to reflect on the academic accomplishments you've already made in your life.
- Ask yourself what advice you'd give to a friend in a similar situation— then follow that advice!

References

Edwards, N. (2004, January). Rediscovering the Creative Heart of Japanese Education: Fostering Intrinsic Motivation through a Love of Language. *The Language Teacher, 28*(1), 19-23.

Hadjioannou, X., Shelton, N.R., Fu, D. & Dhanarattigannon, J. (2007). The Road to a Doctoral Degree: Co-travelers through a Perilous Passage. *College Student Journal, 41*(1), 160.

CHAPTER 2

Dissection of the Elephant: Breaking the Dissertation into Manageable Parts

Barbara F. Shambaugh, EdD; Susanne Beier, PhD; and Robin Buckley, PhD

There are typically five chapters within a dissertation. *Please note, however, it is your responsibility to check with your university's dissertation guidelines to see whether five is the requirement or the suggestion and to look at other successful examples from your program.* Typically, the first three chapters are written as the dissertation proposal. The proposal is reviewed and approved by your chair and committee, and any additional reviewers determined by your specific program, before you can begin collecting data. The last two chapters are written after the proposal has been approved, Institutional Review Board (IRB) approval has been granted, and data has been collected and analyzed to complete the study. The following outline lists and describes the essential parts of each dissertation chapter. Remember to use this outline as a guideline rather than a *have to* list.

WORKSHEET: Dissertation Outline
Title Page
Approval Page
Abstract [*title only at this time*]
Dedication
Acknowledgements
Table of Contents
Lists of Tables
Lists of Figures

Chapter 1: Introduction

Introduction
Background
Problem
Purpose
Significance
Nature/Scope of Study
Research Question, Hypothesis
Definition of Terms
Assumptions, Limitations, Delimitations
Summary

Chapter 2: Literature Review

Introduction
Literature Review
Conclusion
Summary

Chapter 3: Methodology

Introduction
Research Method and Design
Population and Sample
Data Collection Procedures
Survey/Questionnaire [*validity and reliability—if one is used*]
Study Validity [*internal and external*]
Data Analysis Procedures
Summary

Chapter 4: Results

Introduction
Purpose Statement
Organization of Chapter
Review of Data Collection Procedures
Preparation for Data Analysis/Preliminary Analyses
Data Analysis of Each Variable
Graphic Displays of the Data
Description of Results and Conclusions
Summary

Chapter 5: Conclusions, Implications, and Recommendations

Introduction
Problem Statement
Purpose Statement
Methods
Limitations
Ethical Dimensions
Research Questions/Hypothesis
Conclusions
Implications
Recommendations
Future Research
Summary

References
Appendix [*use as needed*]

Chapter 1

1. Introduction—This is where the general topic is introduced.
2. Background—This where you explain why the dissertation problem is important and addresses a social concern or theory.
3. Problem Statement—This is where you introduce the problem you want to study. I like the Cause-Effect rule. What happened (cause) that resulted in a problem (effect).

   Example: A program for relocating spouses is offered by the relocating employees' company. Workshops are offered and individualized sessions are scheduled.

   Result: No one attended the sessions.

   In this example, the problem is that the employee's spouses did not attend programs offered to ease their relocation with their spouse and family. The specific problem is why did they not attend?

4. Purpose Statement—This is where you will state what it is that you want to find out and why. This section also includes the design of your study (to be explained in more detail in chapters 5 and 6). It is also where you will identify the population of your study. Using the example above:

The purpose for the researcher would be to find out what happened. Why did no one attend? The researchers would want to explore whether it was because the participants (spouses) were afraid that if they shared their personal feelings about the upcoming move and uprooting of their family, it would get back to their spouse's employer and would make him/her look less of a dedicated employee.

5. Significance of the Study—This section will identify why this study is important or needed. What contribution would it make to society?
6. Definitions—This is the section where you will identify terms. For example, an educator will be very familiar with the term IEP, yet someone not in the field will not know this means Individual Education Plan.
7. Limitations—In this section, you will identify limitations such as lack of availability of your participants. For example, if you want to interview teachers, you will have to work around school vacation schedules if you are interviewing them on site.
8. Summary—This is where you summarize your key points of this chapter, and it ends with a transition narrative introducing chapter 2.

Chapter 2: Literature Review

In this chapter, you will introduce a review of the current literature related to your dissertation. This review must be thorough, includes appropriate citations, and includes gaps in the research literature, if there are any. Your discussion must include depth and present an analysis of the literature, not a simple listing of sources. In other words, don't create a book report within chapter 2 in which you summarize articles. Instead, you must integrate and synthesize the research through comparison, contrast, and analysis. The end of this chapter should include conclusions resulting from your literature analysis.

Chapter 3: Research Methods

In this chapter, you begin with restating the problem and purpose statement. It will include the appropriateness of the Research Design, (qualitative versus quantitative). Also, it will include the Data Collection Process, Data Analysis, Rationale, and reviews of the population of the study. Your discussion should present an in-depth analysis of the research design instead of a simple listing of what you used.

Institutional Review Board (IRB)

Now that you have completed chapters 1 through 3, you will have a complete proposal. Are you now home free and beginning your actual research and data gathering? NO, you can't! Before you begin to gather data and write chapters 4 and 5, you need to obtain Institutional Review Board (IRB) approval. What is an IRB review?

No research including human subjects can be conducted without first obtaining IRB approval. This approval is granted by the Office for Human Research Protections and provides leadership in areas of welfare and well-being of subject involved in human research (OHRP website).

Here are two questions you will want to ask yourself whether your study will need IRB approval.

1. Does your study involve living human beings (direct or indirect involvement)?
2. Are you systematically collecting or analyzing data with the intent to generalize new knowledge?

The IRB is responsible for ensuring that the federal guidelines about ethical research are implemented appropriately in research projects at their institution so that participants are protected and informed about their research involvement. Participants deserve to know the risks and benefits of their research participation, and it is essential for you, as a new researcher, to carefully consider the ethical implications of your proposed research. Participants can be harmed, and institutions and researchers can experience serious consequences (e.g., loss of funding, halting research, etc.) when research is not conducted in an appropriate manner following legal and ethical guidelines. This means that no research involving human subjects should be conducted (even collecting pilot data) without IRB approval. It is in everyone's best interest to learn about the IRB guidelines and follow them carefully.

The specific forms, process, and IRB members vary somewhat across institutions, so you are advised to work with your chair and the IRB office at your institution to understand what is expected of you as a researcher. You will likely interact with the IRB through the initial approval of your project before you start data collection, and through a renewal process for ongoing studies. So, as you develop your proposal, carefully consider the ethical issues and become familiar with the specific institutional policies and resources of the IRB at your university. Make sure you have the most current guidelines, checklists, and forms from the IRB. For example, the IRB often has specific templates for informed consent, organizational permissions, confidentiality statements, and other documents that you can use for your particular study. These items will help you ensure that you address issues like describing and documenting the informed consent process, confidentiality issues, risks and protection of human subjects, your study population, and other key issues in your proposal and appendices. Consult with your chair about the IRB process before completing/submitting your forms so that the IRB review goes as smoothly as possible. Check with the IRB office to find out about the schedule for submitting forms and the length of review times so that you can plan accordingly on your timeline. Sometimes, the length of review depends on the complexity of the research and the use of specific vulnerable populations. Don't be surprised if the IRB review process results in some additional work and revisions to your proposal. Take these revisions seriously so that you are conducting your research in an ethical way.

Note: For your reference, here is the URL link that will explain in more detail how the IRB Review works: http://answers.hhs.gov/ohrp/categories/1562.

Chapter 4: Data Analysis (Results)

In this chapter, you will present the findings from the data gathered. Your findings need to be clearly and succinctly identified. Specific information needs to be provided so your reader can easily understand how you gathered the data and the results of that data. Remember that in this chapter, you are not interpreting or discussing your results; you are simply and clearly reporting them!

Chapter 5: Conclusion and Future Recommendations

In this chapter, you will summarize what was presented in chapter 4 with one additional component: why would someone care? How does it affect society? How did your study provide anyone with new knowledge? You will also need to include recommendations for future researchers. In other words, if you had to do it all over again, what additional type of research would you want to do to address your research topic? Replicate the study at a later date to see if the data is still applicable? Expand your study geographically?

HHS.gov. Frequent Questions, (2012). NA http://answers.hhs.gov/ohrp/categories/1562

CHAPTER 3

A Proposal That Sails

Ron Hutkin, PhD

Introduction

The purpose of this chapter is to discuss how the dissertation proposal can sail through a review or sink. Although the proposal typically consists of the first three chapters of the dissertation, chapter 1 sets the stage for the remainder of not only the proposal but also the dissertation. However, before we can drift out of the harbor to develop the proposal, you need to identify your dissertation topic.

Will It Float: Topic Selection

You are at the point in the doctoral journey where you have achieved the status of doctoral candidate. Being a doctoral candidate typically means that you completed all the coursework for the doctoral degree, passed the comprehensive exam, and demonstrated competency in research tools such as statistics and/or foreign languages. CONGRATULATIONS . . . now what are you going to do about your dissertation? Maybe you already have a lot of ideas floating around that would make a perfect dissertation topic. These ideas probably came from your course

Selecting your topic

Don't choose things because they are easy or what you think you are supposed to do.

Look around you.

Start by making a list. What do you care about?

Consider problems in your organization, society, or the world at large.

Choose something that adds to the body of knowledge.

Don't commit the Nobel laureate or undergraduate research paper error. (Cone, J.D. & Foster, S.L., 2003, p. 27)

topics and papers, germinal, seminal, and current literature you reviewed, and discussions with your fellow students and dissertation chair and committee members. How do you decide what topic to select for your dissertation?

The objective is to build a case for that perfect idea that will stand up to a rigorous scholarly or peer review. In other words, will your concepts and ideas hold water? Just as good plumbing is watertight, good scholarly writing will hold water and will float through the calm and rough waters of the proposal development and review process.

Starting and changing topics many times wears you down, and you will not be able to move forward. Start with the identified problem, identify the gap, and pursue the historical and recent literature with a vengeance. Before you start to write your proposal, it is helpful to consider the following questions, and review your ideas with your chair. Some programs require a prospectus or concept paper before you write your proposal (see appendices A and B). Either of these documents allows you to clearly define the main points of a proposal and have your research idea approved by individuals identified by your university. This approval process may be incorporated within a class or may involve a meeting with your chair and committee members. Check with your chair and program about the right approach. At the very least, carefully considering these issues (see question worksheet later in this chapter) before you start writing your proposal will help you have a coherent plan.

Keep in mind that your topic should make a difference within the body of literature and, ideally, to those within your study population. In other words, your topic should not simply be an extension of your master's thesis topic. On the other hand, your dissertation is a requirement to get you those initials after your name, so you don't need to tackle solving world hunger in your dissertation. Once you have those doctoral initials, you can go out and change the world . . . prior to that, tackle a dissertation research topic that is manageable and doable.

WORKSHEET: Identifying a topic

What do you want to be an expert in?

_____

_____

_____

What are you most interested in?

_____

_____

_____

What would your role models want you to do?

_____

_____

_____

What important questions do you want to answer?

_____

_____

_____

Would answers to these questions interest a particular community?

_____

_____

_____

What subjects can "ire you up and sustain your interest?

_____

_____

_____

What general subject areas interest you?

_____

_____

_____

Will It Sail?

Whether or not a proposal will sail through rigorous scholarly review depends on a number of factors. What can you do to help insure success in sailing and navigating through unknown waters? Preparation, attention to detail, and clarity are important factors. One way to prepare for writing a proposal is to look at other proposals from other universities as well as your institution. You will see a good deal of variation in format, style guide (e.g., APA), scholarly language, length of paragraphs, and number of sentences in a paragraph. Some institutions may also have their own format guide or a checklist for the components of each chapter. The variations aren't wrong, but you need to adhere to the guidelines and accepted format of your specific university.

> *Writing a dissertation is like learning a new language. The more you allow yourself to become familiar and get immersed in the language of dissertation and scholarly writing, the easier it will become.*

As you review other dissertations, you can develop or augment an existing guide or checklist to use for your proposal. A list of typical headings or subheadings such as Problem Statement, Purpose Statement, Research Questions, Significance of the Study, and others that appear in dissertations will also help answer some questions in regard to the sequence of each chapter's sections (refer to the outline in chapter 2). Also be sure to pay attention to grammar and syntax in your review of other documents. You may have an excellent proposal, but if the grammar and syntax are not at the doctoral level, the wind may come out of your sails sooner rather than later.

In your quest to be a scholarly writer, it is a good idea to avoid reference to self. While using the terms *the writer* or *the researcher* may seem very academic and scholarly, they should be avoided because they detract from the objectivity of your writing. In other words, reference to self may be likened to stating your opinion. In a proposal, your opinion and experience does not get you very far. The proposal is intended to be an objective and unbiased approach to a problem that has significance to the field of knowledge. As you've probably already heard, or will very soon, your opinions, observations, and experiences don't count at this point in your research.

Clarity and brevity are also important parts of scholarly writing. Some students have a tendency to write so much that the true intent becomes blurred and confusing. In reading several hundred proposals, I have read problem statements that occupy two to three pages of valuable space in chapter 1. My reaction was "I don't know what the problem of the study is because the text was too long and lacked clarity." Shorter problem statements have a tendency to be clearer and say more than what was said in several pages. In scholarly writing or informal writing, it is more difficult to be brief than to be wordy. In practice, a good rule of thumb is *less text and fewer words—more clarity and meaning.*

Model for Success

The pinnacle of success is getting the proposal and then the dissertation approved. Is there a secret or magic formula for success? Since most of us do not have magic wands, we need something more practical. In the previous section, the concept of using or creating a checklist of the sections was discussed. One way to develop your own self-rating checklist is to review a number of completed dissertations and do an analysis of the chapters and sections within each. As you create multiple drafts of your proposal, you can do a self-evaluation of the content, the clarity, the grammar, and the scholarly writing before sending it to the full committee for review.

Committee members like to see a clean, edited copy that is well formatted, with chapters having the appropriate length. As a student, you can determine the appropriate length of chapters by reviewing other dissertations. You may determine that an average page length for chapter 1 is about twenty to twenty-five pages, chapter 2 about thirty-five to fifty-five pages, and chapter 3 about fifteen to thirty pages. Of course these are approximations, but they may help you determine if you are significantly under or over the average length for the proposal chapters.

Man or Woman Overboard

So here you are, ready to submit your proposal for review by your chair and committee. You are confident that you have done a great job on the proposal. You get the proposal back and you can barely make out your own writing among all the corrections and comments! The chair or outside reviewer summarizes the review with a comment like *not approved* or tells you the proposal needs major revisions and edits. There is a good chance that if you are human, you will feel somewhat depressed and think that you have been thrown overboard.

Let's look a little deeper at some typical comments. In most instances, when a proposal is returned, not accepted, or not approved, here are the common reasons:

- "After reading the problem statement, I do not know what you are intending to study."
- "Why should we care about the problem?"
- "The problem statement, purpose statement, and research questions are not aligned."

Overall, these comments all focus on one issue: *lack of clarity in the foundational parts of the proposal.*

One hint to avoid potential comments such as these is to give the reviewer a red flag as to what your problem and purpose statements are. For example, "The general problem of this study is . . ." or "The purpose of this qualitative-method study with a phenomenological research design will be to . . ." or "The purpose of this quantitative-method study with a correlational research design will be to . . ." As simplistic as these openers sound, your chair, committee member, or reviewer will have no doubt what you are considering for your problem and purpose statement.

You have to throw out all the creative writing strategies you've learned since elementary school and become comfortable with the redundancy and specificity necessary in scholarly writing. This kind of clarity and brevity will pay big dividends during the review cycle. Instead of feeling like you have been thrown overboard, you will feel like you are the captain of the ship.

The Heart and Soul

Let's visit the importance of the Problem Statement. Most scholars, practitioners, and leaders agree that the *Problem Statement* is the heart of the dissertation proposal as well as the completed dissertation. As we've already discussed, the concept of brevity and clarity are again of primary importance in writing the problem statement.

A model that has proven successful is to cast the Problem Statement in three paragraphs. A suggested length for each paragraph is about eighty words (remember, however, this is just an approximation). In the first paragraph, a discussion of the general context of the proposed problem is appropriate. The second paragraph typically states the specific problem. As we discussed earlier, some students will use that exact wording and start the paragraph with *The specific problem of the proposed study is* . . . Remember that inserting statistics or numbers from research to support your problem statement is an easy way to enhance the power of this statement. Using a citation from a credible source will also support your identified problem as based in objective fact, rather than your own subjective observations.

In the third paragraph, you will discuss the method, design, population, and geographic location relevant to your study. Then the paragraph can be rounded out by indicating where the study will take place, the proposed data collection instruments, and who will participate in the study. Here are a few examples of a third paragraph that meet the criteria:

> This quantitative method study with a correlational research design will address the specific problem and research questions as well as tested the hypotheses. Survey data will be collected using the Watson-Glaser Critical Thinking Appraisal Form S (WGCTA Form S), and the Leadership Practices Inventory (LPI), developed from the conceptual framework of a transformational leadership model created by Kouzes and Posner (2003). The Nurse Practitioner Demographic Tool developed by Rich (2005) will also be used to gather additional relevant data.

> A qualitative modified Delphi research design will be used to address the specific problem. Data for the recommendations will be generated from three surveys and the consensus of a diverse expert panel. Fifteen experts within the educational field and ten experts within the skilled trade workplace who reside in rural Ontario, Canada will comprise the

panel. The results may be germane to policy and decision makers, and educational leaders in the province of Ontario.

Crafting the problem statement with this model will result in success. A brief and clear problem statement will also provide a good segue to the purpose statement. In the purpose statement, the discussion will be an expansion of the method, design, population, and geographic location. The readers of the purpose statement will also want to know why the method is qualitative rather than quantitative and vice versa.

> The purpose of this nonexperimental, qualitative, phenomenological research will be to explore the phenomena of the perceived barriers that prevent the upward mobility of midlevel women in decision-making positions through their lived experiences. Data, which will include the women's perceptions, beliefs, and understandings, will be collected during an interview. Interviews will use open-ended questions and a purposeful sampling strategy among twenty or more women in community colleges in Maryland. The analysis is inductive in that it will seek to discover the premises and categories that emerge from the data (Patton, 2002).
>
> Qualitative methods are appropriate to capture detailed and in-depth information from a small sample of individuals (Patton, 2002). A qualitative approach is appropriate when little is known about a specific concept or "central phenomenon" (Creswell, 2005, p. 45). Therefore, a phenomenological approach is suitable for this study. Phenomenology focuses on "exploring how human beings make sense of experience and transform experience into consciousness . . . how they perceive it, describe it, feel about it, judge it, remember it, and make sense of it, and talk about it with others" (Patton, p. 104).
>
> The primary source of knowledge according to phenomenology is perception (Moustakas, 1994). Perceptions translate into a comprehensive description of the lived experiences of individuals in relation to a central phenomenon, which allows the researcher to unearth underlying themes of meanings (Gibson & Hanes, 2003). The meanings captured could add understanding to the literature regarding the barriers experienced by midlevel women.

So, if the problem statement is the heart of the study, the purpose statement is the soul.

Don't Fret

The importance of the problem and purpose statements may seem overwhelming and can be if not put in the proper context. Many students approach the problem statement as a simple task that can be written in a few minutes. On the contrary, writing a good problem statement may take hours of drafting, redrafting, writing, and rewriting. But don't fret because it is part of the process to get that problem statement to the point where it will hold water and you will sail through your reviews, rather than finding yourself at the bottom of the ocean.

Students who have an approved dissertation proposal will tell you that the problem statement was drafted or revised as many as twenty times. Some changes resulted from lack of clarity, some from the review of literature, and some from changing the method and design. Whatever the reasons, perfect problem statement takes time and patience, as well as research and scholarship at the doctoral level. Can you do it? You bet, but you will need some good objective reviews from people who are interested in your success. Each review helps you get that much closer to a well-designed proposal.

Feedback is a gift!

Connecting the Cells

From the previous discussions, you can start to see how not only the sections of the chapters, but also the chapters themselves, are related to each other. Each chapter builds on the next with chapters 2 and 3 of the proposal and chapters 2, 3, 4, and 5 of the dissertation all referring back to chapter 1. So the importance of having a matrix or evaluation system to self-evaluate your work is important. Your committee will also appreciate that you took the initiative to develop an evaluation system that has criteria or cells that relate to the chapters, particularly in regard to chapters 1, 2, and 3.

While a checklist with cells is not as common for chapters 4 and 5, you need to have a vision of what will be in chapters 4 and 5. You will write chapters 4 and 5 after the proposal receives two approvals: academic content and human subjects' research. The human subjects' research approval is typically granted by a representative of your university's Institutional Review Board (IRB). (This part of the process was discussed in chapter 2.) *Remember that you cannot collect data until the proposal receives these two approvals.* Many students do a pilot test of a questionnaire instrument or a survey instrument. It is important to remember that doing a pilot test is considered collecting data. *Collecting any kind of data from live subjects is a very serious error and could be a showstopper in the proposal/dissertation process.*

Cellophane or Cellopain

Cellophane refers to transparency and clarity in the dissertation proposal or completed dissertation. Cellopain refers to the hurt you will feel when your proposal is returned by your committee or outside reviewers as not approved or needs major changes. There have been instances in which proposals have been in the *not approved* or *needs major revisions* category multiple times. The major reasons can be academic quality, writing quality, or a combination of the two. In the event your proposal is not approved multiple times, the easy, but even more painful route is to give up. Here are a few suggestions that may help you:

1. Take a deep breath and let yourself *quickly and briefly feel the negative emotions* that come with disappointment. (I often tell my mentees to set a timer and give themselves ten minutes to deal with their anger, depression, and self-doubt. The more time and energy wasted on being stuck in that negative rut, the more time it will take to overcome those feelings and finally begin work.) After that . . .
2. *Move on!*
3. Do a quick determination to make sure the *fit between you and your chair* is still there (see chapter 7 regarding the chair and committee).
4. Create a change matrix (see sample at end of this chapter). A change matrix is a valuable tool for both you and your committee, which helps organize your revisions. As you receive feedback, enter the information into your change matrix and update it with your revisions. This helps you to keep track of where and when you make changes. You might decide to offer the change matrix to your committee members at each draft submission so they can quickly review those areas that required editing.
5. After you've done all this, *get to work* and address the feedback from your chair and committee.

ABD Cell

Now that you are a doctoral candidate, you should eliminate the *almost-a-degree* letters ABD—short for *all but dissertation*—from your thinking and vocabulary. You probably know some friends or colleagues who are ABDs. You might want to visit them about why they did not complete the doctoral journey. Some likely answers are life happens, ran out of time and money, career and job issues, or family issues.

Our goal in this book is to have you complete the doctoral journey. There are some underlying reasons that contribute to being an ABD, and you have to decide not to let any of these reasons affect you!

Now, you are essentially on your own and the one responsible for taking charge to write your proposal. You can decide whether to allow this to make you feel all alone, or empowered to be the director of your show. Your dissertation chair will be there, on the sidelines, to help, but remember that in many cases dissertation chairs are very busy people and may not be available at every, critical moment. Try to set up a regular time to communicate with your chair. Regular communication helps dissipate the feeling that you are not alone as an independent scholar. Setting up a communications network of others who are in the proposal writing stage also helps. Face to face contact is the best, but telephone or communicating by Skype are valuable as well. The worst thing you can do is to avoid communication.

Luck or Scholarship?

There have been several suggestions in the chapter to either make or modify a checklist such as the one at the end of chapter 2 for evaluating the proposal by self or the committee. Such a checklist should be composed of several parts related to the chapters, as well as the format and presentation of the proposal. Some typical parts of a checklist might include chapters 1, 2, and 3, the front pages such as the title and table of contents, the references, the appendices, and the overall quality of scholarly writing.

When all the pieces of the proposal are in the right place, through careful preparation and attention to detail, chances of having a successful review on the first reading or maiden voyage of the proposal will be greatly improved. When your proposal is approved, you will have achieved the pinnacle of success. Some contend that getting the proposal approved is the most difficult part of the journey. So with an approved proposal in hand, or on your computer, you should have smooth sailing for chapters 4 and 5.

How about a graphic or picture? *A sailboat would be appropriate.*

Change Matrix: TITLE OF DISSERTATION						
Student: Chair: Committee member: Committee members:						
Change #	Input date	Source of change	Reviewer's requested change (including original location—chapter and page)	Changes made	Location of change (chapter and page)	Date completed

CHAPTER 4

The Literature Review

Linda de Charon, PhD

Chapter 1 of the dissertation, the introduction to the study, is followed by chapter 2, the literature review. For some, the thought of conducting a literature review is daunting. It seems like a Herculean effort to survey the literature. It is hard to even get started. Some students feel like they have to read every article that is remotely related to their topic; thus, it is hard to know where to start or where to stop. The end result is typically procrastination. For others, reading is not the problem. They could read all day long. They are voracious readers. In fact, one interesting idea or article just seems to lead to another. Time flies by. But at the end of the day (and six cups of coffee later), the facts and ideas and inspiration they got from reading all of those papers is not organized in their head or on paper in any meaningful way (but they did enjoy the coffee!). For others still, they do a good job of reading relevant articles in their particular realm of interest, can speak meaningfully about the issues in that area, and even have some notes and references to support their thoughts. However, they don't have the bigger picture, having confined their reading to one narrow area. They are unaware of some of the fruitful ideas, controversies, and approaches that could be gained from reading more broadly.

The literature review is one of the greatest challenges for doctoral students because the enormous amount of literature available can quickly become overwhelming. It can be confusing to identify the relevant information, and it can be difficult to organize the information in a meaningful way. The review of the literature must include both depth and breadth. Students usually do not have much of a problem developing an appropriate amount of *depth*—they usually include a suitable level of detail on each topic. However, it is often difficult to recognize the appropriate *breadth* of the literature review for a study—the span of topics that are appropriate to support the study.

> *Necessary characteristics of a literature review:*
>
> *depth and breadth*

Whether you are having a hard time getting started, have read but can't remember or organize all the facts you learned, or only have a tunnel vision of your topic, there is hope. Yes, the process of conducting a literature review is a major task in research, but it is much more manageable if you 1) start early and proceed steadily, 2) document and organize well along the way, and 3) follow the guidelines in this chapter to develop both depth and breadth of knowledge. In fact, whether or not you realize it, your literature review process begins the day you start reading articles about your topic of interest. The skills you use to conduct a good literature review are part of writing any paper for any doctoral class. Surveying and synthesizing the literature helps you to define your own interests and details for your research study. And, as a lifelong learner, you will continue to need to search and summarize research literature, whether you are planning your next research grant project, publishing a scholarly review paper, or preparing a new presentation for the class you teach. This chapter is designed to assist you with writing a thorough and thoughtful literature review—recognizing the appropriate breadth of topics to include in your literature review and organizing the information effectively.

Purpose of the Literature Review

The literature review serves an important purpose in the dissertation as it must support the significance of the problem and expand on the theoretical framework that is discussed in chapter 1 of the dissertation. The literature review should be exhaustive and typically should synthesize at least fifty references, although 100 to 150 might be more representative. Chapter 2 of the dissertation is often expected to range from about thirty to fifty pages in length; however, the length of the literature review is based on the study. The literature review should present the information with a certain degree of fluidity, integrating the various sources almost effortlessly.

The literature review should support the need for the study and the significance of the study. It should support that there is an existing problem, and that the research is a worthwhile endeavor. The discussion should persuade the readers that there is clearly a gap in knowledge that needs to be addressed, and that the research will add to the existing body of knowledge.

The discussion must also convince the readers that the topic and its foundational theories have been thoroughly reviewed in depth and breadth. The literature review should include classical references, citing the historical experts in the field and the original theorists associated with the topics. Note that although original theories are often referred to as *seminal*, the gender-neutral and therefore more appropriate term is *germinal* theories. The literature review should also include current, contemporary perspectives on the topics. In addition, you must discuss previous studies related to your topic and explore any controversies within the field of study. Taking a walk off the beaten path of literature often leads to interesting discoveries!

Getting Started

Preparing for the literature review should begin as quickly as possible within the doctorate program. Doctoral programs typically consist of several core courses that require extensive reading. Use the reading opportunities to your advantage by beginning an annotated bibliography to briefly document any references that may be applicable to your dissertation. Annotations should consist of the full reference information followed by a paragraph or two of the key points of the article such as the method, design, and key findings. Often all of the relevant information can be extracted directly from the abstract of an article.

A key to developing a comprehensive literature review is first identifying all of the topics relevant to the study. A common error in the literature review is focusing too narrowly on the specific topic under investigation, resulting in a literature review that meets the depth requirement, but lacks breadth. The mind-mapping activity in this chapter—Activity 4.2—will help you to define appropriate topics.

> *A common error is to focus just on the main topic. Think outside of the box! Consider all relevant topics.*

Annotated Bibliographies

As you define your study topics, organize your annotated bibliography according to the various topics. Collecting appropriate information on relevant references encountered during the doctorate journey is one of the most important, yet, easiest steps that can be taken to facilitate the literature review process. Creating an annotated bibliography will provide a synopsis of current research accomplished on your topics.

Simply collecting sources for a bibliography is somewhat beneficial; however, much of the value of an annotated bibliography is the process of writing the annotations. This process requires thoughtful reading and use of critical thinking to identify the following: a) the scholarly appropriateness of the source and b) the key points of the information. The annotated bibliography should include bibliographic information needed for the dissertation references and citations and must provide a concise summary of each of the references.

The purpose of an annotated bibliography is to capture the key points of an article for your future use. Annotations should be limited to one or two paragraphs that identify the key elements of relevant journal articles and dissertations. Whenever applicable, the research design, findings, implications, and recommendations should be included in the annotation. For sources that are not based on research, simply include the main ideas of the source.

For example, a qualitative study on the construct of career and money as depicted by contemporary singer/songwriters might include analysis of lyrics from ABBA song "Money, Money, Money" (Andersson, & Ulvaeus, 1976), Pet Shop Boys' song "Opportunities (Let's Make Lots of Money)" (Tennant & Lowe, 1985), and Jackson Browne's song "The Pretender" (Browne, 1976). An initial step would be to create annotated bibliographies on these three sources to capture the meaning conveyed by each source.

ABBA's song "Money, Money, Money" (Andersson, & Ulvaeus, 1976):

I work all night, I work all day, to pay the bills I have to pay
Ain't it sad
And still there never seems to be a single penny left for me
That's too bad
In my dreams I have a plan
If I got me a wealthy man
I wouldn't have to work at all, I'd fool around and have a ball

These lyrics could result in the following annotated bibliography:

Andersson, B., & Ulvaeus, B. (1976). "Money, Money, Money" [ABBA]. *Arrival* [CD]. Stockholm, Sweden: Polar Music.

This song written by the two male members of ABBA and performed by the entire group including two female members in Sweden in the mid-1970s reflected the struggles of the working woman to succeed financially. The lyrics reflect a desire for a life without the need for employment. The lyrics imply that attainment of this aspiration could be accomplished only through marriage to a man of means.

Pet Shop Boy's "Song Opportunities (Let's Make Lots of Money)" (Tennant & Lowe, 1985):

I've got the brains, you've got the looks
Let's make lots of money
You've got the brawn, I've got the brains
Let's make lots of money

These lyrics could be captured as:

Tennant, N. & Lowe, C. (1985). "Opportunities (Let's Make Lots of Money)" [Pet Shop Boys]. *Please* [CD]. London, UK: Parlophone/EMI.

This song written and performed on the initial album released by the male duo in the UK in the mid-1980s revealed a vision to become financially secure. The lyrics imply that while one group member was seen as intellectual, the other was perceived as the more attractive member of the band. The combination of intellect and attractiveness was depicted as presenting the capability for financial success. Seemingly, their vision of potential opportunity was accurate since according to *The Guinness Book of Records* (1999), the Pet Shop Boys are the "most successful duo in UK music history" (p. 228).

Jackson Browne's song "The Pretender" (Browne, 1976):

> I'm going to be a happy idiot
> And struggle for the legal tender
> Where the ads take aim and lay their claim
> To the heart and the soul of the spender
>
> Say a prayer for the Pretender
> Who started out so young and strong
> Only to surrender

An annotation for these lyrics might be:

Browne, J. (1976). "The Pretender" [Jackson Browne]. The Pretender [CD]. Burbank, CA: Asylum/Electra.

> This song written and performed by a solo American artist in the mid-1970s illustrates the enthusiasm of youth yielding to assimilation into corporate America. The lyrics imply that advertising agencies tend to lure people to focus on attaining material goods, to the detriment of their own character. The implication is that many surrender to lifestyle focused on making money for the purpose of conspicuous consumption.

Developing annotations is an important step toward creating a literature review, but each reference is still viewed individually at this point. An example of how these three sources might be developed into a comprehensive and cohesive literature review is provided later in this chapter, in the *synthesis of sources* section. But before you begin integrating references, you should create a blueprint. The following section describes the initial step for developing an outline of your literature review.

Theoretical Framework

A starting point for all research methods is to begin with the theoretical or conceptual framework of the dissertation, typically discussed in chapter 1 of the dissertation. The theoretical framework may be defined as the set of theories that underpin the study. In contrast, the conceptual framework may be defined as the interrelationship between the various elements associated with the planned research. Therefore, a conceptual framework may be used in a quantitative study to describe the known associations between the variables, or in a study that is based on an existing conceptual framework that was developed during a previous study.

As stated, the theoretical framework should provide a set of theories that underlie the study. The framework begins with a broad theoretical foundation that serves as a basis for this study. The theoretical framework discussion should begin very broadly with the foundational theory and narrow toward theories related to the specific research purpose—think of moving from the top of a V toward the tip.

The following figure depicts a sample hierarchy of theories. The depicted framework is associated with a study of the relationship between the introversion/ extroversion and intuition/sensing continua of the Myer-Briggs Type Instrument® and doctoral success. The Myer-Briggs Type Instrument® was created in 1943 based on the "germinal psychological types" theory, developed by Carl Jung in 1921. Therefore, the foundational theory is Jung's psychological types, followed by the Myer-Briggs Type Instrument®, then introversion/extroversion and intuition/ sensing, and finally personality and doctoral success. Keep in mind that the actual theoretical framework is simply text; the purpose of the V is only a mental model used to depict that the literature should begin broadly and end with a narrow focus on your specific topic. In Activity 4.1, you will be developing a framework for your study.

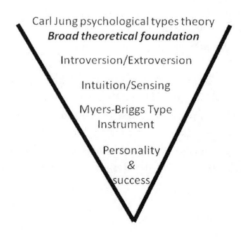

Carl Jung psychological types theory
Broad theoretical foundation

Introversion/Extroversion

Intuition/Sensing

Myers-Briggs Type Instrument

Personality & success

Broad Theoretical Foundations

As examples of broad theoretical foundations, studies of human behavior may be based on social theory, motivation theory, cognitive dissonance, levels of consciousness, multiple intelligences, change theory, or resistance to change; and organizational studies may be based on organizational systems theory, organizational learning theory, or retention theory. Consider such germinal theorists as Durkheim, Fayol, Festinger, Freud, Gardner, Jung, Lewin, Maslow, McClelland, Mintzberg, Schein, Senge, Taylor, or Weber. Technological or environmental research might be rooted in general systems theory as initially developed by Bertalaffy. Studies rooted in education may draw from a rich tapestry of germinal studies, including the observational learning theory (Bandura), hierarchy of learning (Bloom), constructivist theory (Bruner), experiential learning (Dewey or Rogers), development theory (Erikson), conditions of learning (Gagne), social development theory (Vytkotsky), moral development (Kohlberg) or behaviorism (Pavlov, Skinner, Thorndike, or Watson).

As you develop your theoretical framework, consider how your study aligns with existing germinal theories. Review the various theories briefly described above and whether your study has origins in any of these constructs. Another method for identifying a relevant foundation for your study is to review the theoretical framework section of published dissertations related to your topic.

> *Reviewing dissertations and articles on your topic is a great way to start identifying associated theories*

WORKSHEET 4.1: Identify Your Theoretical Framework

- Write the purpose statement of your study.

  _____
  _____
  _____
  _____

- Review the statement and consider the broad area(s) under which your study falls.

  _____
  _____
  _____
  _____

- Identify germinal theories and theorists associated with those areas.

  _____
  _____
  _____
  _____

- *Hint:* Although Wikipedia should not be considered a scholarly source, it can be useful for identifying the history of information and identifying original theorists. However, once the references are identified, it is important to locate and read the primary sources.

  > Wikipedia can be useful for identifying original theorists and germinal sources, but then read the original sources.

- Consider any additional theoretical underpinnings related to your study.

  _____
  _____
  _____
  _____

- For quantitative research, also consider your dependent, independent, and intervening variables.

  _____
  _____
  _____
  _____

- Use the following template to depict the hierarchy of theories to be used in your study.

  _____
  _____
  _____
  _____

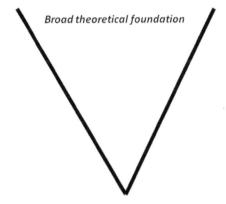

Broad theoretical foundation

Locating References

Locating appropriate sources to support your research is an important part of your doctoral journey. When reviewing potential references to include in your dissertation, remember to view all sources through the lens of critical thinking. Remember that locating and reading primary sources is crucial and germinal references, such as primary references for foundational theories, can typically only be found in brick-and-mortar local libraries or university libraries. Current sources should be peer-reviewed (also known as *refereed*) journal articles.

University libraries will often include online access to general and specialized databases. Most database search engines will include an option to limit the search to peer-reviewed journals. Another option to identify peer-reviewed sources is *Ulrich's Periodicals Dictionary*. This source can be found in brick-and-mortar libraries and may also be available as a resource within online university libraries.

Current theory should include contemporary experts in the field and should include *cutting-edge* thought, philosophies, and ideas. The literature review current overview should reflect the state of the topic at present. All viewpoints, perspectives, and controversies must be included to familiarize yourself and the reader with the existing state of the field.

Guidelines on Developing the Literature Review

You should cite primary sources rather than rely on and cite secondary sources. For example, you read an article on observational learning theory written by Deeming and Johnson (2009) that cites Bandura (1962). It is certainly easier to extract a citation directly from this current article on Bandura's germinal theory and use a secondary citation "(as cited in Jones, 2011)." However, secondary source citations should be limited to books out of print or unavailable and sources written in a foreign language with no English translation published. The expectation for dissertations is that you should cite the primary source (Bandura, 1962). Therefore, you should locate, read, and cite Bandura's original work.

Direct quotes and block quotes should be used very sparingly. Using too many direct quotes is often viewed as a form of plagiarism, and direct quotes should be used only to support your own thoughts and writing rather than in place of it. Any quotes should be carefully selected and used when only the author's original words can capture the essence of the statement. Also, make sure to cite your direct quotes appropriately, using APA formatting. However, more often, you should *paraphrase* by restating the passage. Paraphrasing can be accomplished by reading a passage and then reiterating the meaning in your own words, without the original quote in front of you.

Avoiding Bias

References should be selected based on rationality and reason rather than emotion or passion for supporting a specific position. A common error for novice researchers is to select references and quotes that support their personal position rather than to remain open to the entire expanse of literature on the topic. Bias must be completely avoided throughout the entire dissertation process, including the literature review. Remember that the purpose of a dissertation is not to *prove* and support your position on a topic—it is to *research* the topic without bias. Critical thinking requires including all relevant literature and analyzing the sources open mindedly, which includes presenting all sides of a topic.

> *The objective of a dissertation is not to prove and support your position on a topic—it is to research without bias*

Mind Mapping

Mind maps can play a vital role in developing a comprehensive literature review. Research problems are typically multifaceted and it is imperative to identify all of the dimensions related to the study. Mind mapping helps to create a structure to organize the typically complicated and complex literature review process. The process of developing the map is a good tool for brainstorming the various topics relevant to a planned study. The maps can help researchers recognize important areas, challenge conventional thinking and assumptions, and uncover unique perspectives that contribute to the significance of the study.

The process of mind mapping can be accomplished either manually or using one of the many software programs available via the Internet. A search of free mind-mapping tools will result in at least ten various software programs available for this task, but consider allowing your creative juices to flow by developing your map manually. Using a manual process allows you to focus on the mind map itself, rather than on learning the software process.

A mind map can be developed as a diagrammatic representation of the theories, topics, subtopics, and variables. The mapping exercise is used to generate, organize, and visualize the relevant topics. The insights uncovered during the mind mapping process can enhance efficient literature review development practices.

ACTIVITY 4.2: Mind Mapping Your Topic

- Begin with a large piece of paper and a few colored pens or pencils.
- Write the purpose of your study in the center of the diagram and circle it. This will be the core of the mind map; everything else will be represented in a radial manner from this central concept.
- If you have identified the research questions, write those questions on radial lines that emanate from the core circle. If you are still uncertain about the research questions, this is a good time to consider options.
- Remember that the aggregate of the research questions should fully address the purpose. Consider whether your research questions fully address the purpose, or possibly addresses topics beyond the scope of the purpose.
- If the research questions are beyond the scope of the purpose statement, then refine either the purpose or the research questions.
- If your study is quantitative, add radial lines from the research questions to indicate how the hypotheses align with the research questions.
- Add smaller bubbles for each of the quantitative variables and indicate how they are aligned with the hypotheses. Use lines or colors to show the interrelations between the variables, such as dependent, independent, and intervening variables.

- Add the broad area(s) under which your study falls to the mind map, including the germinal theories and theorists.
- Add any additional theoretical underpinnings that you identified as during the theoretical framework activity. At this point, you should have a good depiction of the classical or historical aspect of your literature review.
- Consider the current or contemporary counterparts for each of the germinal theories and add those to the diagram.
- Consider any cutting-edge findings or controversies and add those to the mind map.
- Now consider your research instrument—the quantitative survey or interview questions that you will be using. Review the instrument for any key words that should be added to your mind map.
- If you are creating your own instrument, also use the mind map to ensure that your survey or interview questions encompass all of the ideas that you are trying to capture.
- Include the context of your study, such as the population under study and the geographic location.
- Use color or symbols to group related concepts. The colors or symbols will help you identify the interconnectedness throughout the mind map. Define all of the concepts as key words and consider any synonyms to those key words.

The fluidity of the map allows visual cues that can be missed with a simple hierarchical listing. Identifying concepts and key words provides a list for database searches. The mind map allows you to consider whether you have included all of the important concepts, facilitates your understanding of how the various concepts and theories are related, and guides your literature search. Also importantly, the visual map will allow you to identify what can be *excluded* from the scope of your study. The following figure depicts the first several steps of developing a mind map. However, do not constrain your map by just including the major elements. Ensure that you tap into your creativity while developing your map and use the exercise to really think outside of the box.

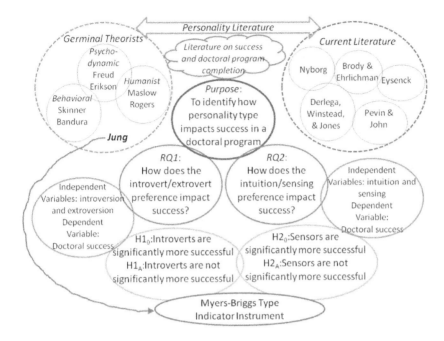

Defining an Exhaustive Literature Review

Once the scope of the proposed research has been identified using the mind mapping technique, you can review your collective annotated bibliography to decide what resources to include and to exclude within your literature review. Your literature review should be comprehensive, yet within the well-defined boundaries of the scope of your study (see chapter 2 regarding scope of study). An annotated bibliography will facilitate an understanding of what has already been accomplished in the field, and how your proposed research can fill an existing gap in the literature.

Synthesis of Sources

Keep in mind that the information should not simply be a sequence of information regarding each topic. It is important to *synthesize* the information by comparing and contrasting the references. Although the annotated bibliographies focus on individual references, the literature review should focus instead on specific topics, comparing and contrasting perspectives from various references on that topic.

> *Rather than describing each source individually, compare and contrast what the sources have to say on the topic*

Revisiting the following annotations from earlier in this chapter, we will now look at how this information can be synthesized into an integrated section on career and money as depicted by contemporary singer/songwriters. Again, below are the three annotations presented earlier in this chapter:

Andersson, B. & Ulvaeus, B. (1976). "Money, Money, Money" [ABBA]. *Arrival* [CD]. Stockholm, Sweden: Polar Music.

> This song written by the two male members of ABBA and performed by the entire group including two female members in Sweden in the mid-1970s reflected the struggles of the working woman to succeed financially. The lyrics reflect a desire for a life without the need for employment. The lyrics imply that attainment of this aspiration could be accomplished only through marriage to a man of means.

Tennant, N. & Lowe, C. (1985). "Opportunities (Let's Make Lots of Money)" [Pet Shop Boys]. *Please* [CD]. London, UK: Parlophone/EMI.

> This song written and performed on the initial album released by the male duo in the UK in the mid-1980s revealed a vision to become financially secure. The lyrics imply that while one group member was seen as intellectual, the other was perceived as the more attractive member of the band. The combination of intellect and attractiveness was depicted as presenting the capability for financial success. Seemingly their vision of potential opportunity was accurate since according to *The Guinness Book of Records* (1999), the Pet Shop Boys are the "most successful duo in UK music history" (p. 228).

Browne, J. (1976). "The Pretender" [Jackson Browne]. *The Pretender* [CD]. Burbank, CA: Asylum/Electra.

> This song, written and performed by a solo American artist in the mid-1970s, illustrates the enthusiasm of youth yielding to assimilation into corporate America. The lyrics imply that advertising agencies tend to lure people to focus on attaining material goods, to the detriment of their own character. The implication is that many surrender to a lifestyle focused on making money for the purpose of conspicuous consumption.

Based on these three sources, the following is an example of a synthesis:

Career and Money as Depicted by Contemporary Singers/Songwriters

In the 1970s and 1980s, a few singers/songwriters from the United States and Europe wrote and sang about working for a living and their aspirations of success. While some depicted success as financial gain (Andersson & Ulvaeus, 1976; Tennant & Lowe, 1985), another viewed the pursuit of money as defeat—a surrender of heart and soul (Browne, 1976). Browne, an American, implied that some people lose sight of the meaning of their lives, choosing to focus on making money solely for the purpose of conspicuous consumption.

Viewed from the perspective of gender, Andersson and Ulvaeus (1976) described the struggles of the working woman and her desire for a life of leisure without the need for employment. Andersson and Ulvaeus implied that attainment of this aspiration could be accomplished only through marriage to a man of means. In contrast, as two males new to the music industry, Tennant and Lowe (1985) contended that the combination of their intellect and handsomeness could be the key to their future financial success. As recorded in *The Guinness Book of Records* (1999), this duo was correct in their prediction of success as the Pet Shop Boys are the "most successful duo in UK music history" (p. 228).

Note that the discussion of the individual sources is interwoven or synthesized into a literature review. When developing your literature review, include plenty of headings for each topic. Just focus on synthesizing relevant sources within that topic. Taking the topics in bite-sized chunks will help you to not become overwhelmed by the literature. The following section discusses how to organize the literature section by section.

Organizing the Literature

A common issue that doctoral students face is the seeming inability to develop a comprehensive, inclusive literature review. Done correctly, it should be very easy to meet the typical thirty to fifty pages. The following sections describe expectations for each section in the literature review.

Introduction Section. The introduction section should not include a separate heading. Briefly reiterate the topic and scope of the study, and then introduce the literature review. Also include an overview of the chapter section.

Documentation Overview. Following the chapter 2 introduction, include a section heading such as *Documents Researched* or simply *Documentation.* One common option for this section is to include key words searched. Another option is to include a table of search findings, such as the number of journals, books, and dissertations reviewed for each topic addressed in the literature review. Either method should work well, but remember that if the table exceeds a page, it must be moved to an appendix.

Formatting the Literature Review. The topics within the literature should flow from broad, general topics and narrow toward the specific topics related to the purpose of the study. Much of the theoretical framework and the information should be formatted as a *V*. The main section of the literature review should include a historical overview of the various topics, a current overview of those same topics, and any contemporary topics. Previous studies related to the purpose of the study should also be discussed to provide support for the significance of the study being proposed. The following discussion provides detailed information on developing these sections.

Historical Overview. Begin with a historical overview section that includes separate subheadings for each topic from the theoretical framework. Begin with the broadest theoretical area that provides the foundation for the theoretical framework. Also review your mind map for any additional topics that should be included. For quantitative studies, ensure that each study variable is discussed. A good method for delineating between historic information and current information is to include all references over five years old within the historic section. Also ensure that any controversies between theorists are described, but do not indicate support for either position. The literature review must be unbiased.

Current Overview. Follow the historical overview section with the same sequence of subheadings as you used in the historical overview section. The current overview should provide a synopsis of contemporary literature on each of the topics or variables. Review your mind map for any additional topics that have been introduced in the literature within the last five years. The current overview should include recent dissertations and cutting-edge information within the field. Again, include any controversies between current theorists, while avoiding the perception of bias.

Previous studies. The literature review must include a focus on what has already been accomplished within the field of study. The description must include methods and designs used to previously study the problem and reveal controversies between the researchers, also defined as tensions in the literature. The literature review must present a critical analysis of the existing research, describing the scope and the limitations of studies that have already been accomplished.

Literature Gap/Significance of the Proposed Study. The discussion of previous studies and what has already been accomplished within the field of study should provide a basis for the gap in the literature. Describe what still needs to be uncovered, and how your proposed study will assist in closing the current gap in the literature. Discuss how your proposed method and design may be a significant contribution to knowledge within the field of study.

Conclusions. The conclusions section should consist of conclusions that you have derived based on your analysis of the literature. The discussion should include the interconnections between the knowledge that currently exists in the field. The section should also place your proposed study within the context of the existing literature.

Chapter 2: Summary. The summary section should briefly summarize the key points of the chapter. It is, of course, important to include citations throughout the summary. Finally, include a transition to chapter 3. Remember to include transition statements at the end of all chapter summaries.

WORKSHEET 4.3: Literature Review Criteria

Once you have developed your draft literature review, compare the contents to the checklist criteria to ensure that you meet the expectations. Review each statement and self-score each item on a 1 to 4 scale, with 1 being the lowest score. Use your scores to identify what areas of your literature review should be improved to fully meet the criteria.

Literature Review Criteria	*Score*
1. The scope of the study is clearly stated	
2. The literature review search criteria is clearly stated	
3. The sources are scholarly and peer reviewed	
4. The review includes historical context	
5. The review includes current research that has been accomplished in the field	
6. The review includes critical analysis of current literature	
7. The literature review includes appropriate breadth for the topic	
8. The depth of the discussion includes controversies and tensions in the field	
9. The literature is synthesized appropriately	
10. The review describes the scope and limitations of recent studies	
11. The discussion includes clear support for the significance of the proposed research	
12. The discussion includes clear support for the method and design of the proposed research	
13. The review includes conclusions derived from the analysis of existing literature	
14. The summary includes key points and includes a transition to chapter 3	

Relevance of the Literature Review to the Dissertation Process

It is important to recognize how the literature review chapter fits into the broader picture, how chapter 2 supports the other dissertation chapters. During the proposal phase—chapters 1 through 3—the literature review provides the foundation for both of the other chapters, chapter 1 and 3. The literature review supports the significance of the study—why the proposed research is important and how it may contribute to the existing body of knowledge. The literature review also briefly describes how the proposed method and design compare to previous research.

This comparison creates the basis for the chapter 3 discussions on appropriateness of the selected method and design.

Following the completion of the data collection and analysis, the literature review becomes an important element in chapter 5. In that final chapter, the focus is on the implications of the findings, and conclusions and recommendations. In the implications of the finding section, the study finding must be compared to and contrasted against existing literature—the literature described in chapter 2.

> *Keep in mind that you will need to compare and contrast your study findings to the literature in chapter 5.*

Summary

Although the literature review is often one of the greatest challenges for novice researchers, specific steps can be taken to simplify the process. Developing a comprehensive literature review requires identification of the topics relevant to the study, beginning with the theoretical or conceptual framework of the dissertation. Germinal references, such as primary references for foundational theories, will likely require a trip to a brick-and-mortar library.

All sources must be assessed using critical analysis, and current sources should be peer-reviewed and include contemporary experts in the field. Bias must be avoided; the purpose of a dissertation is not to support a position but to research the topic open-mindedly. Research problems are typically multifaceted and systematic development of a mind map to diagrammatically represent the theories, topics, subtopics, and variables can be very helpful to reveal all of the dimensions of the study. The map allows identification of both what should be included in the scope of the study, and what can be excluded from the scope.

Beginning an annotated bibliography as soon as possible and adding to that database during the doctoral program will provide a practical synopsis of current research. Key items to include in the annotations include the research design, findings, implications, and recommendations. Accomplishing the thirty to fifty pages required for the literature review can be quite easy, but it must be more than a sequence of information on each topic; it must synthesize the information.

The review must include what has already been accomplished within the field of study and support the significance of the proposed study. The literature review provides a foundation for dissertation chapters 1, 3, and 5. The review of existing literature becomes the source for comparison of your study findings against what exists in the field today; therefore, the literature review is the basis for supporting that your study contributed new knowledge to the field.

CHAPTER 5

Qualitative Research

Kelley A. Conrad, PhD

In chapter 3, you set sail on your dissertation by creating effectively worded problem and purpose statements. In chapter 4, you learned how to conduct a literature review by identifying relevant literature and collecting it in an annotated bibliography. Using critical reasoning, you saw how to explore the structure of the literature using mind mapping and finally how to focus your discussion using the *V* model, moving from theoretical foundations to specifics related to your study. With this work completed, you are ready to revisit your initial statements of the problem and purpose for your research as you move to consideration of your method.

Note that you did not start your statements of your problem and your purpose with the method you planned on using. This follows the approach of serious researchers who begin any study with the issues they want to investigate, develop their thoughts into problem statements or research questions, examine the purposes of their research, and only after all that, choose a method to use.

Today, there is an abundance of research designs available to any serious researcher. Before a person gets caught up in the details of one specific design, it is wise to appreciate the big picture of methods and analysis. There are three basic approaches that underlie all methods: qualitative, quantitative, and combinations of those two in mixed methods approaches.

Qualitative Research

Data collected for qualitative research is in verbal and textual form. Virtually all research begins as qualitative investigations. The researcher begins by asking questions of themselves and then of others. Often these questions originate from common sense and informal observations. When no one else has

Qualitative research is a conversation with a purpose.

72

explored a problem involving other people, an excellent place to begin is to have a purposeful conversation with those people of interest. When we want to be more systematic and contribute more than hearsay, we need to be more systematic. There are three major families of qualitative methods based on the focus of the research, each of these allow us to approach our conversation from a slightly different perspective depending on our purpose. *Grounded theory* or *interpretative phenomenological analysis* explores the phenomena of lived experiences by looking for commonalities from which to develop a theory describing the phenomenon. *Ethnographic* research collects verbal data as a way of developing an understanding of the culture that exists within a group of people; this can be a small, well-defined intact group or an entire culture. *Biographical* or narrative research collects data from and about individuals.

Quantitative Research

The simplest definition of quantitative research is research that collects data in numerical form. If you just asked yourself, "Where do I get the numbers?" You have just realized most quantitative research requires some preliminary work either to identify the characteristics you want to tally or to use various measureable outcomes to assess

> *Quantitative research is often intervention research, manipulating and measuring results.*

changes. Tally studies that collect descriptive data usually without manipulation are called nonintervention research. Assessment studies where variables are experimentally manipulated and measured are called intervention research. The scientific method is a systematic approach to finding and confirming general rules that describe, explain, and predict outcomes. The dominant approach in the scientific method is experimental research, and most experimental research involves some quantification through measurement.

Mixed Methods Research

The third major method is the mixed-methods research, combining elements from quantitative research with elements from qualitative research in particular

> *Mixed-methods research combines qualitative and quantitative approaches in particular patterns to increase generalizability.*

patterns to develop a fuller and more generalizable understanding of the question being investigated. There are two major mixed methods strategies. The one named *mixed methods* simply combines the two methods in particular purpose selected patterns in order to develop detailed research understandings. The second mixed-methods approach is action research. This is a special focus within mixed methods used when individuals study situations in which they are also active participants.

In chapter 3, you set sail on your dissertation journey by developing your problem and purpose statements. Next, in chapter 4, you explored the literature to find theories and research that were related to your problem and purpose. With that preparation, you are now ready to begin work in earnest on your research method.

How Your Problem and Purpose Determine Your Method

Revisit your problem and purpose and make sure both are clearly stated. Your theoretical and research support for both should be logically related and current. Review your problem statement. Is it in the form of a question that will be addressed in verbal terms? Or is it in the form of an outcome that can be measured and described with numbers? If it is the former, you probably have identified a study that will use qualitative approaches. If it is the latter, you probably have a study that will use quantitative approaches.

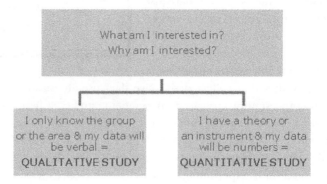

Qualitative Research

Where do you begin if no one has studied the phenomenon in which you are interested? Or do you begin when the research you can find does not seem relevant to your research question? You can begin in the same place curious minds have always started, by asking questions of others. This is the essence of qualitative research. It is the starting point of informed inquiry and the search for answers.

Qualitative research has been defined as

> any type of research that produces findings not arrived at by statistical procedures or other means of quantification. It can refer to research about persons' lives, lived experiences, behaviors, emotions, and feelings as well as about organizational functioning, social movements, cultural

phenomena, and interactions between nations. Some of the data may be quantified as with census or background information about the persons or objects being studied, but the bulk of the analysis is interpretative. (Strauss & Corbin, 1998, pp. 10-11)

Qualitative research methods have enjoyed considerable popularity beginning in the 1990s and continuing today. There are a number of books devoted to describing various qualitative approaches and designs. Five major approaches have emerged as somewhat more popular. This chapter will focus on those. The five major approaches are:

Grounded Theory
Phenomenological Research
Case Studies
Narrative Research and Biographies
Ethnographical Research

Qualitative research methods depart from simple conversation because as scientific endeavors, the methods are governed by an underlying logical progression that is one of the hallmarks of the scientific method and similar in structure to that found in more formal quantitative research methods. The strengths of qualitative methods are that they are more open to the unknown or unexpected and have few, if any, constraints or presuppositions.

> *The strengths of qualitative methods are that they are more open to the unknown or unexpected and have few, if any, constraints or presuppositions.*

Qualitative Analysis—Stair Steps to Success

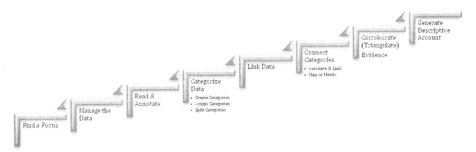

Although original qualitative investigations were essentially guided conversations, as qualitative research has gained popularity, it has become more disciplined. Our "stair steps to success" model illustrates the underlying discipline of most qualitative studies. This discipline connects formal qualitative research to the scientific method and makes qualitative results comparable to those of quantitative studies. Exploring these steps can help you develop an overview of what will be involved in virtually any qualitative study.

Find a Focus

Many qualitative researchers are motivated by their desire to create positive change (Kidder & Fine, 1997) and their desire to reflexively consider the consequences of their dedication to that desire (Finlay, 2002). Your focus is stated in your research question or questions. The way you state your research questions will lead you to different qualitative approaches.

Your research question(s) states the focus for your study and is the guide for the method you select.

Research Question	Features	Qualitative Approach
What are the experiential components of being in love?	Explores the common structure of the lived experience being in love	Phenomenonology
How do people who have HIV/AIDS make personal sense out of the way others respond to them when they discuss being in love?	Explores personal meaning and sense making for those who share the experience	Interpretative Phenomenological Analysis
What structure exists when people tell stories about falling in love?	Explores common narrative patterns that contribute to sense making	Narrative Analysis
What factors influence how people develop the feeling that they are in love?	Explores explanatory structure to understand patterns, factors, and influences on love	Grounded Theory
How do people talk about being in love?	Describes the interactions and descriptions of being in love	Discursive Theory

Manage the Data

Collecting, organizing, and archiving qualitative data can be a significant challenge. You will discover qualitative data can be voluminous. Not only do you need to collect and validate verbatim transcripts of your interviews, you also need to track the sources of the data you use in your analyses. This can be a complicated and time-consuming task. Today, there are computer programs like NVivo, Atlas.ti, and

SPSS that support the research by making it easier to keep track of the individuals who made the comments while the researcher conducts the analyses.

Read and Annotate

Qualitative analysis usually requires the researcher to read and reread the narrative data. Often it is necessary for the researcher to read all the data at least three times. First, to develop an overview and sense of the entire body of data collected. A second reading is used to categorize the data in the effort to identify underlying structure. This is often repeated until the researcher is confident of the categories and accuracy of the coding.

> *Qualitative analysis often requires you to read all your data at least three times.*

A final reading is needed to collect key ideas and validate them with appropriate quotes. Annotation during these readings is the way you keep track of your incidental thoughts about the data or your reactions to it. This process of annotation is termed *coding in* or *bracketing*. In some qualitative methods, IPA for example, the annotations may be quite extensive since they document the analytical thoughts of the researcher.

Categorize the Data

Data categorization is the way themes emerge. The researcher looks for rational categories or themes that can be used to sort and organize the interview comments.

Create Categories
Categories are like piles or buckets full of related comments. As you read your data, you watch for identifiable units in the comments. When you find a comment that seems important as a possible component of structure, you label it and start a file in which you will place all similar comments.

Assign Categories
As you read through all your data, you categorize all the meaningful comments into the emergent structure. You use existing categories when the comment fits and create new categories when no existing category works.

Split Categories
Because the structure is *emergent,* it is not unusual to discover some of your initial categories were too general and are collecting many comments. In these cases, you sort through all the comments and see if it makes sense to split that large category into several.

Link Data

After all the data has been sorted into coherent categories that are internally consistent, you step back and look at the data with an eye to building a structure. This will provide the basis for your theoretical or descriptive summary of your data.

Connect Categories

Associate and Link

Analysis may uncover clusters of categories that can be meaningfully associated and or linked. Laying these out is one way to begin to map a theory describing the phenomenon.

Map or Matrix?

Two common methods are used to display the final structure. Maps are used when there is a hierarchical structure or other clusters of categories. A matrix is used when no such structured relationships are clear, but the categories are.

Corroborate (Triangulate) Evidence

If your qualitative research stops after collecting and categorizing the data, it remains mainly opinions. True, you have invested a lot of time and effort finding structure in the verbal comments, but you have not demonstrated that your structure will apply to other similar situations involving the phenomenon. To validate your structure, you need to triangulate it. This means corroborating it by finding a similar sample, collecting data from that sample, analyzing the data, and then matching the new structure to the original. When the two match, you have triangulated your analysis. Some studies will collect several kinds of data and triangulate the results by seeing if the two analyses yield similar structures. Of course, if you do this, you are still working with only one sample of subjects, so any generalization will be limited.

Generate Descriptive Account

The last step in qualitative analyses is to write the descriptive account. This part of a qualitative analysis is usually the longest part of the paper. In addition, the tradition of qualitative research has been that the descriptive accounts are written with greater sophistication than is true for most quantitative studies. When you choose to do a qualitative study, you need to be prepared

> *Qualitative research results are corroborated through additional evidence triangulating the results.*

to spend more time and energy in clearly describing your results and how they justify your commitment to the research.

Recommended Reading and References

Brizuela, B. M., Stewart, J. P., Carrillo, R. G. & Berger, J. G. (2000). *Acts of Inquiry in Qualitative Research*. [Reprint series no 34]. Cambridge, MA: Harvard Educational Review

Creswell, J. W. (1998). *Qualitative Inquiry and Research Design: Choosing among Five Traditions*. Thousand Oaks, CA: Sage.

Denzin, N. K. & Lincoln, Y. S. (Eds.) (2011). *The Sage Handbook of Qualitative Research* (4th ed.). Thousand Oaks, CA: Sage.

Finlay, L. (2002). Negotiating the Swamp: The Opportunity and Challenge of Reflexivity in Research Practice. *Qualitative Research, 2*, 209-230.

Flick, U. (2009). *An Introduction to Qualitative Research* (4th ed.). London, England: Sage.

Kidder, L. H. & Fine, M. (1997). Qualitative Inquiry in Psychology: A Radical Tradition. In D. Fox & I. Prilleltensky (Eds.), *Critical Psychology*. London, England: Sage.

Patton, M. Q. (2002). *Qualitative Research & Evaluation Methods* (3rd ed.). Thousand Oaks, CA: Sage.

Smith, J. A. (Ed.) (2008). *Qualitative Psychology: A Practical Guide to Research Methods* (2nd ed.). London, England: Sage.

Strauss, A. & Corbin, J. (1998). *Basics of Qualitative Research: Techniques and Procedures for Developing Grounded Theory*. Thousand Oaks, CA: Sage.

Wertz, F., J., Charmaz, K., McMullen, L. M. & Josselson, R. (2011). *Five Ways of Doing Qualitative Analysis: Phenomenological Psychology, Grounded Theory, Discourse Analysis, Narrative Research, and Intuitive Inquiry*. New York, NY: Guilford Press.

Qualitative Research Design Map

As you might expect, qualitative research is a rich tradition of investigation and like other approaches has developed a number of approaches. For this reason, it is important to consider your approach and the implications it has for your research in qualitative research.

Tesch (1990) developed a comprehensive map of the various types of qualitative research. While we cannot discuss all of these in this book, Tesch's diagrams graphically illustrate the evolving traditions in qualitative research.

The place to begin your selection of method is with the research question you defined. Different traditions of investigation have evolved based on research questions addressing four aspects of communication about phenomena. The four areas are language characteristics, discovery of regularities, comprehension of meaning, and reflection. When you can visualize each of these and the qualitative methods that have developed to investigate each, the decision of which method to choose becomes a relatively easy process of following the diagram.

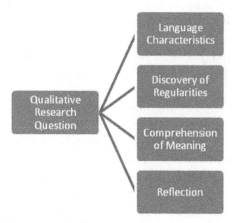

Figure: Major Qualitative Research Categories (Tesch, 1990, p. 72)

When qualitative research explores the domain of language characteristics, the first choice is to select one, either communication or culture as the focus. When communication is selected, the next choice is between content analysis (either content or process explorations) or ethnographic communication and discourse analysis. When a cultural focus is selected, the next choice is whether to explore it cognitively using ethnoscience or interactively using structural ethnography or symbolic interactionism. These relationships are illustrated in the following diagram based on Tesch's (1990) descriptions.

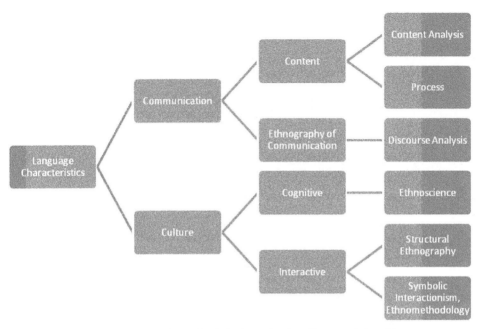

Figure: Qualitative Research Methods for Investigating Characteristics of Language
(Tesch, 1990, p. 72)

The second focus for qualitative research is the most popular. When you seek to discover regularities in the way individuals experience and describe their lived experiences, this is the family of qualitative methods you select from. There are two major groups of approaches depending on whether your research question leads you to simply identifying the elements and possible connections or whether your research question challenges you to discern and map identifiable patterns in the descriptions. The following diagram illustrates the various qualitative methods you can use as alternative strategies to explore subtle variations in the focus of your research question.

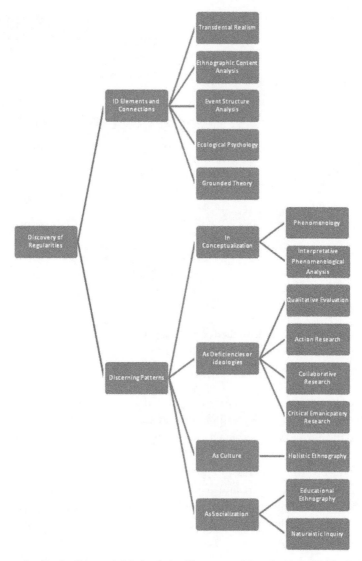

Figure: Qualitative Research Methods for Discovery of Regularities (Tesch, 1990, p. 72)

Of course, you may be interested in meaning and not simply communications. Meaning is a more elusive quest but one that challenges researchers to develop understanding instead of only mapping structure and patterns. As a more inferential approach, searching for meaning will require you to be highly engaged in your analysis. This can be difficult or impossible to do if you are too emotionally involved. For this reason, it is advisable to avoid areas where your passions are particularly strong. The two major groups of qualitative analysis focused on comprehension of meaning are thematic analysis and interpretative analysis. These are presented below.

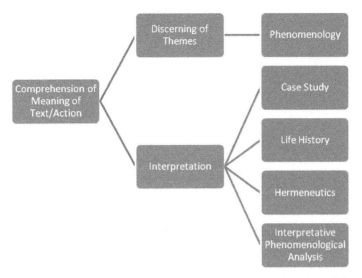

Figure: Qualitative Research Methods for Developing Comprehension of Meaning
(Tesch, 1990, p. 73)

The final methodological family focus derived from qualitative research questions is reflection. When you ask a research question that explores reflexive insights developed as a result of the participant's lived experiences, you can select from three qualitative methods: educational connoisseurship, reflective phenomenology, or heuristic research. This methodological focus is displayed in the following figure.

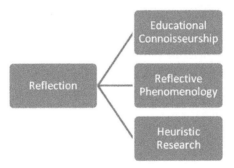

Figure: Qualitative Methods for Developing Reflexive Understanding (Tesch, 1990, p. 73)

All figures based on Tesch, R. (1990). *Qualitative Research: Analysis Types & Software Tools* (pp. 72-73). London, UK: RoutledgeFalmer.

At first, the maps of the various qualitative methods may seem complicated. In reality by moving from left to right and basing your decisions

Method maps of qualitative research approaches help you select the most appropriate approach to address your research question and purpose.

at each point on your clearly stated research question, the diagrams should lead you to the most appropriate qualitative method to use for your study. You use the first chart to select the major focus expressed by your research question. Next, you move to the one diagram that maps that focus and move through it to the most appropriate qualitative method. With your choice made, you can now study the method in depth so you can design your study following the appropriate standards and current state-of-the-art practice.

We don't have the space in this book to describe all the qualitative methods you could select using the diagrams just discussed. However, you have probably recognized that a few of the methods are more popular. We will describe the grounded theory, phenomenology, case study, narrative, and ethnographic in more detail. An excellent resource for exploring qualitative research methods is the *Sage Research Methods* database. This research methods tool provides access to over 100,000 pages of Sage's book, journal, and other reference content with a focus on methodology. Information about this resource is available from *www.srmo.sagepub. com*

Grounded Theory

Grounded theory is a qualitative method used to discover regularities through the identification of elements and connections distilled from the descriptions of participant lived experiences.

Essence of the Method

Grounded theory is a way of extracting theory from a data set that describes a social reality. The theory emerges from the data itself, rather than from outside sources, and therefore, is highly dependent on the nature of the circumstances within the social reality reviewed. Glaser and Strauss created the approach, developing a highly structured data gathering method that focused on predicted characteristics within the data. Strauss and Corbin (1998) relaxed the data collection structure, allowing for the emergence of the data from within the data gathering process, rather than on prescribed focal points for the data review. The theory emerges from the data collection and interpretation techniques deployed in the investigation process. In this way, it is seen as *grounded* in the comments, as they exist.

Strategic Intention of the Method

From a large body of verbal data collected, you will look for themes and patterns in interview data and artifacts. Through analysis and the addition of other data as appropriate, you generate a theory of operation for the phenomena or phenomenon under review. Modeling is central to grounded theory as you aggregate themes and patterns to explain the relationships and connections developing a theory of how participants experience and think about their experiences of the phenomena.

Research Planning and Data Gathering

> *In grounded theory, the theory emerges from the data itself and is dependent on the circumstances and the social reality reviewed.*

Grounded theory requires a robust design, with the research analysis occurring across *sufficient time* with enough data or artifacts to ensure sufficient data for theory building. As a result, what constitutes an appropriate data set will depend on the nature of the study, the complexity of the phenomenon under review, and your ability to identify and synthesize the study findings into a cohesive theory. Careful attention to these features of a grounded theory is necessary in order to assure both a robust study and credible findings and an integrated theory to describe those findings.

Your research proposal for a grounded theory study should include a thorough description of the context of the grounded theory, of the research site, of any artifacts, and the data gathering design. Given the breadth of these studies, informed consent is typically a significant issue, assuring the participants and the organizations involved in the study of their protection.

Recommended Reading and References

Corbin, J. & Strauss, A. (2007). *Basics of Qualitative Research: Techniques and Procedures for Developing Grounded Theory* (3rd ed.). Thousand Oaks, CA: Sage.

Glaser, B. G. & Strauss, A. L. (1967). *The Discovery of Grounded Theory: Strategies for Qualitative Research.* New York, NY: Aldine de Gruyter Publisher.

Goulding, C. (2002). *Grounded Theory: A Practical Guide for Management, Business and Market Researchers.* Thousand Oaks, CA: Sage Publications Publisher.

Locke, K. (2001). *Grounded Theory in Management Research.* Thousand Oaks, CA: Sage Publications Publisher.

Richards, L. (2009). *Handling Qualitative Data: A Practical Guide.* (2nd ed.). London, England: Sage.

Strauss, A. & Corbin, J. (1998). *Basics of Qualitative Research: Techniques and Procedures for Developing Grounded Theory.* Thousand Oaks, CA: Sage.

Using Grounded Theory

Data Processing and Interpretation

What do you do with quantities of verbal data? Just examining the transcriptions of the notes from a qualitative study can be overwhelming. Most of us who have completed qualitative studies remember well the concern we felt when first faced with all those words and the challenge to make some kind of sense out of them. How then can we proceed from our general research interests expressed in our research question and purpose to some kind of meaning? For a while and for some researchers even today, grounded theory is *the way* to analyze qualitative data. Henwood and Pidgeon (2003) described the current approach as

> [a]n *intertwining* of research processes and outcomes—where the process involves the detailed, systematic but flexible interrogation of (a range of) initially unstructured data selected for its close relationship to the problem under investigation and the analytical outcome (often with the powers of formal explanatory theory) combine a demonstrable relevance and "fit" to the substantive problem, phenomenon, or situation under investigation. (p. 136)

Coding Schemes Terminology

Open coding—concepts are identified and their properties and dimensions are discovered in the data

Phenomena—central ideas in the data represented as concepts

Concepts—the building blocks of theory

Categories—the concepts that stand for phenomena

Properties—characteristics of a category; the delineation of which defines and gives it meaning

Dimensions—the range along which general properties of a category vary, giving specification to a category and variation to a theory

Subcategories—unique categories that are reflected and aggregate under topical categories

Axial coding—the act of relating categories to subcategories along the lines of their properties and dimensions

Selective coding—the process of integrating and refining theory

Theoretical saturation—the point in category development at which no new properties, dimensions, or relationships emerge during analysis

Range of variability—the degree to which a concept varies dimensionally along its properties (variation as a component of the design being built into the theory)

Theory—larger theoretical schemes refining the theory (review the scheme for internal consistency and logic, fill in poorly developed categories, and validate the theoretical scheme; what if a case does not fit?)

Coding Process

Ask questions
Make comparisons (see the comparative comparison discussion above)
Look for action/interaction between data points
Justify the themes and patterns by bringing qualitative quotations to explain
Themes and patterns identified. Three to four quotations for each of the themes.
Select patterns that are highly relevant for the qualities or the essence of what
you attempt to describe in the themes identified.

Structure of Report

Chapter 1 identifies the overarching research questions, theoretical framework of the study, and the nature of the grounded theory study. Substantive and/or formal theory generation is identified in the discussion.

Chapter 2 explores the theoretical framework of the study and related literature to the study.

Chapter 3 explores the research protocol, artifacts, and research protocol with qualitative questions identified. A grounded theory must occur over time as it is not sufficient to develop theory for a study period of a short duration. A substantive amount of time must be identified for the study to be able to take on the characteristics of a theory, measuring the phenomena/non over a significant period of time appropriate to the phenomena/non itself.

Chapters 1-3 also serve as your proposal.

Themes and patterns are identified for chapter 4 and supported with relevant quotations from the research data

Chapter 4 is where you identify and aggregate the themes and patterns into your theory, explaining the structure you have discovered.

In chapter 5, you explore the components of your theory and discuss the importance of what you found. You use relevant literature to explain, explicate, and relate the theory presented. It is important for you to explain how your theory adds to the body of literature. If you fail to make a solid connection with existing literature, it is unlikely others will find your conceptualization helpful.

Recommended Reading and References

Birks, M. & Mills, J. (2011). *Grounded Theory: A Practical Guide.* London, England: Sage.

Charmaz, K. (2006). *Constructing Grounded Theory: A Practical Guide Through Qualitative Analysis* (Introducing Qualitative Methods series). London, England: Sage.

Gilgun, J. (2011). Grounded Theory as Open-ended and Adaptable: Three Views (Current Issues in Qualitative Research). [Kindle DX version]. Retrieved from Amazon.com

Gilgun, J. (2010). *The Intellectual Roots of Grounded Theory* (Current Issues in Qualitative Research) [Kindle DX version]. Retrieved from Amazon.com

Henwood, K. & Pidgeon, N. (2003). Grounded Theory in Psychological Research. In P. M. Camic, J. M. Rhodes & L. Yardley (Eds.), *Qualitative Research in Psychology: Expanding Perspectives in Methodology and Design* (pp. 131-155). Washington, D.C.: American Psychological Association.

Phenomenology

Phenomenology is a qualitative method used to discover regularities by discerning conceptual patterns distilled from the descriptions of participant lived experiences. A recent variation of phenomenology is interpretative phenomenological analysis (IPA). Created by Smith (1996), IPA has a distinctive psychological focus while other phenomenological research has a more sociological focus. Babbie (2001), a sociologist, uses the term *field research* to capture the focus of observing social life in its natural habitat and the richer understanding obtained. Your choice of what strategy to use is determined by the research question you asked and your purpose for doing the research.

Essence of Phenomenology

Phenomenological research explores the essence of phenomena. Phenomenology is a philosophical approach to human experiences. Husserl (1931) founded phenomenology as the careful examination of experience as it occurs. He advocated we should, "go back to the things themselves." This has evolved in popular practice to making a researcher's interpretations central to the description of the phenomena. Moustakas (1994) described the researcher's perception as the way the "truth of things" is established (p. 57). In contrast, Dukes (1984) described verification of perceptions by including the researcher's lens and an outside reviewer's lens. Although not all phenomenologists agree on the essence of the method, phenomenology studies small groups of carefully selected individuals in an effort to discover patterns of meaning and relationships.

Strategic Intention of Phenomenology

From a large volume of narrative data collected, the researcher will look for themes and patterns in interview data, artifacts, and their analysis and other data points as appropriate, to generate a theory of operation for the phenomenon under review. As with grounded theory, modeling becomes a feature of phenomenology, as themes and patterns are aggregated to explain the relationships and connections for a theory of operation. The philosophical base used for the approach to the interpretation determines what shape the results will take—whether they will be more focused on capturing the essence of the experience or be more interpretive based on the perceptions of the researcher.

> *Phenomenology extensively studies small groups of carefully selected individuals exploring their lived experiences of a selected phenomenon as directly as possible.*

Research Planning and Data Gathering

Phenomenological inquiry requires a disciplined data collection, with the research analysis occurring across *sufficient time* and *experiences* to ensure a robust data set for theory building. As a result, what constitutes an appropriate data set will depend on the nature of the study, the complexity of the phenomenon under review, and their viability to be synthesized into a cohesive theory.

The research proposal should include a good description of the context of the phenomenon with a thorough description of the research site, artifacts, and the data gathering strategy. A statement of the artifacts, longitudinal and breadth of the study must be thoroughly explored in chapter 3 of the proposal. Informed consent is typically a significant issue, assuring the participants and the organization/s involved in the study as to the protection of the organization and research participants in the study.

Interpretative Phenomenological Analysis (IPA)

Interpretative phenomenological analysis (IPA) as a phenomenological approach is focused on how individuals make sense of their personal and social worlds. IPA is focused on understanding the meaning of personal experiences for the individuals. The intent is to understand the person's perceptions rather than producing an objective statement describing the phenomena. Smith, Flowers, and Larkin (2010) described the approach in their book,

> In IPA we are assuming that our data (provided that they permit us access to a reasonably rich and reflective level of personal account) can tell us something about people's involvement in and orientation towards the world, and/or about how they make sense of this. Typically, this requires us to identify, describe and understand two related aspects of a participant's account: the key 'objects of concern' in the participant's world, and the 'experiential claims' made by the participant in order to develop a phenomenological account. (p. 46)

Types of Research Questions

IPA researchers conduct in-depth examinations of the individual participant's lived experiences and how the individual makes sense of those lived experiences. The types of questions IPA addressed are illustrated by the following research questions from IPA studies:

> *It can be said that the IPA researcher is engaged in a double hermeneutic because the researcher is trying to make sense of the participant trying to make sense of what is happening to them. (Smith, Flowers & Larkin (2009, p. 3)*

> How do gay men think about sex and sexuality? (Flowers, Smith, Sheeran & Beail, 1997).

> How do people with genetic conditions view changing medical technologies? (Chapman, 2002).

> What role, if any, do spiritual beliefs play in helping older people come to terms with the death of a partner? (Golsworthy & Coyle, 1999).

How do homeless people describe the impact on their identity? (Riggs & Coyle, 2002).

Recommended Reading and References

Dukes, S. (1984). Phenomenological Methodology in the Human Sciences. *Journal of Religion and Health, 23*(3), 197-203.

Flowers, P., Smith, J. A., Sheeran, P. & Beail, N. (1997). Health and Romance: Understanding Unprotected Sex in Relationships Between Gay Men. *British Journal of Health Psychology, 2,* 73-86.

Golsworthy, R. & Coyle, A. (2001). Practitioners' Accounts of Religious and Spiritual Dimensions in Bereavement Therapy. *Counselling Psychology Quarterly, 14,* 183-202.

Husserl, E. (1931). *Ideas: General Introduction to Pure Phenomenology.* (D. Carr, Trans.). Evanston, IL: Northwestern University Press.

Lyons, E. & Coyle, A. (2007). *Analysing Qualitative Data in Psychology.* Los Angeles, CA: Sage.

Moustakas, C. (1994). *Phenomenological Research Methods.* Thousand Oaks, CA: Sage.

Riggs, E. & Coyle, A. (2002). Young People's Accounts of Homelessness: A Case Study of Psychological Well-Being and Identity. *Counselling Psychology Review, 17,* 5-15.

Smith, J. A., Flowers, P. & Larkin, M. (2009). *Interpretative Phenomenological Analysis: Theory, Method, and Research.* Los Angeles, CA: Sage.

WORKSHEET 5.1: *Interpretive Phenomenological Analysis Worksheet*

Check off each item as it is completed:

☐ 1.   Study phenomenology and select my preferred approach.
☐ 2.   Explore topics
☐ 3.   Select topic
☐ 4.   Describe purpose and research question or questions
☐ 5.   Identify any secondary or theory-driven research questions
☐ 6.   Find an appropriate sample
        Estimate sample size
        Examine constraints like availability, access, ethical constrains
☐ 7.   Plan the data collection
        A.   Appropriate method for collecting the data
        B.   Practice and develop in-depth interviewing
        C.   Develop structure for semistructured interviews
☐ 8.   Conduct the interviews
☐ 9.   Contextualize the interviews
☐ 10.   Transcribe the verbatim record of the interviews.
☐ 11.   Analyze the data
        A.   Read and reread the transcripts
        B.   Make initial notes
        C.   Add descriptive comments: Linguistic comments—
             Conceptual comments.
        D.   Deconstruct participant conceptualizations
☐ 12.   Develop emerging themes
☐ 13.   Search for connections across emergent themes.
☐ 14.   Develop the model that captures the relationships
☐ 15.   Repeat for each case.
☐ 16.   Look for patterns across cases.
☐ 17.   Interpret the results and patterns
☐ 18.   Write the summary report.

Case Study Focus

Stake (2005, p. 443) noted, "Case study research is not a methodological choice but a choice of what is to be studied." "A *case study* is an in-depth description and analysis of a bounded system" (Merriam, 2009, p. 40). A case study is used to comprehend the meaning of text or action through in-depth description and interpretation of the descriptions

> *In case studies the focus of the research is the case itself optimizing the understanding of the case rather than generalizing beyond it.*

of participant lived experiences in a bounded system. That is to say, you may use any of a variety of approaches, but the focus of your research will be *the case itself*. Stake also observed that, while most researchers who study cases name their studies using other labels than case study, some select the name case study as a way of drawing attention to the value of what is learned by studying a single case. If you choose to complete a case study, keep Stake's advice, "to optimize understanding of the case rather than to generalize beyond it" (p. 443). Platt (2007, p. 102) in an excellent overview of the varieties of approaches observed case study "has been both a major category distinguishing complete alternative research styles, and a passing description meaning no more than that the study is of a single case."

Essence of Case Study

Qualitative case study research is a detailed study of the system that is naturally bound by the people, place, experience, or time (Stake, 1995, 2005). An example of the potential value of a single case is the discovery of HIV, which led to the identification of HIV as the cause of AIDS. The history of HIV/AIDS was detailed in an article by Vahlne (2009). Several case studies by Gallo and coworkers in 1980 (Gallo, Salahuddin, Popovic, Shearer, Kaplan, et al., 1984) discovered the first human retroviruses (HTLV-I). Montagnier's research group isolated the virus from a single patient with lymphadenopathy using Gallo's protocol and reported this in 1983. A summary of the previous case studies and an experimental test (Vilmer & Barre-Sinoussi, 1984) by Gallo's group established HIV-I as the cause of AIDS. Different kinds of cases include a single individual, several individuals as a group, a program, an event, selected activities—almost any situation that can be clearly delimited. Some cases are even programs, for example a program of study. Special terms identify the reasons a case is selected. The common component is that a case is a single, identifiable entity defined by boundaries that can be described. If the phenomenon of interest is not clearly bounded, then a case study approach is inappropriate.

Strategic Intention of Case Study

Stake (2005) described the value of case studies as optimizing

> understanding by pursuing scholarly research questions . . . by thoroughly triangulating the descriptions and interpretations, not just in a single step but continuously throughout the period of study . . . [concentrating] on experiential knowledge of the case and close attention to the influence of its social, political, and other contexts. (pp. 443-444)

Case study research has a long history in the field of research, and in educational research, case study has recently experienced a revival (Gomm et al., 2000). According to Merriam (1998), case study is appropriate when one wants to understand the experiences in-depth in a rich, descriptive fashion. Lahman and D'Amato (2006) stated that a case study is persuasive through the details that convince the reader and makes clear the complexity of the case. If one wants the reader to understand how life is for the participants, a case study offers a compelling story. In addition, Morgan (2002) has advocated for focus groups that have a more natural context or feel to them.

Research Planning and Data Gathering

Types of Case Studies

Historical, Observational, Life History (Bogdan & Biklen, 2007)
By researcher interest (Stake, 2005)
Intrinsic Case—selected because the case itself is of interest to the researcher (Stake, 2005)
Collective Case—multiple cases selected for a common relationship to a central issue (Stake, 2005)
Instrumental Case—selected to call attention to a particular issue (Stake, 2005, p. 445)
Collective Case Studies—cross-case, multicase, multisite, and comparative

In a case study, the researcher will collect multiple forms of information in order to triangulate and confirm the observations. It is important the researcher clearly define the situatedness of the case so the unique character is understood. Case studies are unique in another way; other qualitative approaches can be used within the boundaries of a case study.

Method

Stake summarized the case study method in this statement, "Place your best intellect into the thick of what is going on" (2005, p.449). To this he added that "the brainwork ostensibly is observational, but more critically, it is *reflective*" (2005, p. 449). The case study method drawn from the description by Stake (2005) follows:

Case Selection

Choose your case well. It should represent a meaningful representative of the phenomena you are interested in.

Is a single case adequate?
Is a representative sample of cases needed?

Interactivity

Develop an understanding and description of the activity or functioning of the case.

What does the case do?
How do the contexts influence the activities in the case?
How does the case respond differently to complex situations?

Data Gathering

Respond to the challenge of developing and using distinctive expression within a case as the process for detecting and studying the underlying commonality of the phenomenon of interest.

What details can you observe directly?
What details can you learn about by interviewing people who observed or experienced them directly?
What documents describe or record details not directly observed by participants or the researcher?
Does the size of the case require teaming? If so, what is the plan for collecting and coordinating the data?
What patterns are present?

Triangulation

Responsible researchers realize the need to demonstrate the validity of their observations and conclusions. This is accomplished by the process of triangulation.

What alternative perceptions, observations, or documents will clarify meaning or establish repeatability?
In what other ways could the selected case be viewed?

Interpretation

Develop your understanding of the case and the way it illuminates the phenomena of interest.

What assertions or generalizations can be made about the case?

Recommended Reading and References

Bogdan, R. C. & Biklen, S. K. (2007). *Qualitative Research for Education: An Introduction to Theories and Methods.* Boston, MA: Pearson.

Gallo, R. C., Salahuddin, S.Z., Popovic, M., Shearer, G. M., Kaplan, M., Haynes, B. F., et al. (1984). Frequent Detection and Isolation of Cytopathic Retroviruses (HTLV-III) from Patients with AIDS and at Risk for AIDS. *Science, 224,* 500-503.

The SAGE Handbook of Interview Research: The Complexity of the Craft (2nd ed.).Thousand Oaks, CA: Sage.

Holstein, A. B. Marvasti, & K. D. McKinney (Eds.). (pp. 161-176). The SAGE Handbook of Interview Research: The Complexity of the Craft (2nd ed.). Thousand Oaks, CA: Sage.

Platt, J. (2007). Case Study. In W. Outhwaite & S. P. Turner (Eds.), *The Sage Handbook of Social Science Methodology* (pp. 102-120). Thousand Oaks, CA: Sage. doi:10.4135/978184607958

Stake, R. E. (1995). *The Art of Case Study Research.* Thousand Oaks, CA: Sage.

Stake, R. E. (2005). Qualitative Case Studies. In N. K. Denzin & Y. S. Lincoln (Eds.). *The Sage Handbook of Qualitative Research* (3rd ed.) (pp. 443-466). Thousand Oaks, CA: Sage.

Vilmer, E., Barre-Sinoussi, F., Rouzioux, C., Gazengel, C., Brun, F. V., Dauguet, C., et al. (1984). Isolation of New Lymphotropic Retrovirus from Two Siblings with Haemophilia B, One with AIDS. *Lancet, 1,* 753-757.

Narrative Research and Biographies

"Narrative is present in every age, in every place, in every society" (Barthes, 1977, p. 79). Narrative research can be oral or written, specifically elicited (part of an interview) or simply overheard (naturally occurring in conversation), or short (focused on an event), longer (describing a significant event), or extended (describing a person's entire life). The major types of narratives include life history, life story, personal narrative, oral history, testimonial, and performance narrative.

Chase (2005) identified five analytic lenses used by researchers when developing narratives.

Retrospective Meaning Making—You are thinking about the past to develop understanding and to create meaning from experiences. Meaning making is done from the point of view of the narrator. The meaning includes emotions, thoughts, interpretations, and uniqueness.

Verbal Action—Narrative captures action and accomplishments, emphasizing the narrator's voice. Emphasis is on creativity, credibility, believability, and the self.

Bound by Social Circumstances—Narratives can display patterns across individuals representative of different times, cultures, and places.

Socially Situated Interactive Performances—Narratives intended for a specific audience and or for a specific purpose. This type of narrative is shaped by the interaction with the audience, which can include any active listeners.

Narrating the Narrator's Interpretations—Here the narrator applies any of the four previous lenses to themselves and the narratives they have produced.

> *For narrative research, do not think of the interviewee as answering your questions; allow them to tell their stories in their own voice.*

Recommended Reading and References

Barthes, R. (1977). *Image, Music, Text* (S. Heath, Trans.). New York, NY: Hill & Wang.

Chase, S. E. (2005). Narrative Inquiry. In N. K. Denzin & Y. S. Lincoln (Eds.). *The Sage Handbook of Qualitative Research*, 3rd ed. (pp. 651-679). Thousand Oaks, CA: Sage.

Czarniawska, B. (1997). *Narrating the Organization: Dramas of Institutional Identity*. Chicago, IL: University of Chicago Press.

Denzin, N. K. & Lincoln, Y. S. (Eds.) (2000). Introduction: The Discipline and Practice of Qualitative Research. In N. K. Denzin & Y. S. Lincoln (Eds.). *The Sage Handbook of Qualitative Research*, 2nd ed. (pp. 1-28). Thousand Oaks, CA: Sage.

WORKSHEET 5.2: Narrative Interview Process Worksheet

Interview Process

　　Do not think of the interviewee as answering your questions; allow them to tell their stories in their own voice.

Frame the interview as a whole using broad open questions that invite a personal narrative.

Ask only selected open-ended questions.

Stay oriented to the narrator's story and voice.

Attend to the story being told and invite new stories.

Counter the societal belief that "interviews generate useful information" and stories do not. (Denzin & Lincoln, 2000, p. 633).

Avoid asking narrators to compare, abstract, or generalize (Czarniawska, 1997).

Interpretive Process

Begin with the narrator's voices and stories.

Listen first for the *voices within* the narrative.

Avoid thematic classification.

Attend to the *narrative strategy*—the specific way a narrator connects various stories over the courses of the narrative.

Develop or adopt a systematic strategy for listening to and interpreting the complexity within the narrator's voices.

Recommended Reading and References

Clandinin, D. J. (2007). *Handbook of Narrative Inquiry: Mapping a methodology*. Thousand Oaks, CA: Sage. doi:10.4135/9781452226552

Creswell, J. W. (1998). *Qualitative Inquiry and Research Design: Choosing among Five Traditions*. Thousand Oaks, CA: Sage.

Elliott, J. (2005). *Using Narrative in Social Research*. Thousand Oaks, CA: Sage. doi:10.4135/9780857020246

Squire, C., Andrews, M. & Tamboukou, M. (2008). Introduction: What is Narrative Research? In C. Squire, M. Andrews & M. Tamboukou (Eds.). *Doing Narrative Research*. Thousand Oaks, CA: Sage. doi: 10.4135/9780857024992

Strauss, A. & Corbin, J. (1998). *Basics of Qualitative Research: Techniques and Procedures for Developing Grounded Theory.* Thousand Oaks, CA: Sage.

Ethnographic Research

Ethnography uses observation as the principle source of data about social or cultural phenomena. The researcher is working to observe and collect information about the customs of a social or cultural group from patterns in their behavioral exchanges. The typical approach is that of a discursive interview. Some various approaches are popular enough they are considered schools of ethnographic thought. Examples include structural functionalism, cultural anthropology, feminism, and postmodernism (Atkinson & Hammersley, 1994). The final report is called an ethnography and is typically a lengthy, often book-sized description.

> *In ethnography the researcher is working to observe and collect information about the customs of a social or cultural group from patterns in their behavioral exchanges.*

Ethnographic Interviews

In ethnographic interviews, the researcher and participant typically know each other and have an existing relationship. The resulting emotional content needs to be considered in the analysis. Most ethnographic interviews are impromptu and brief. They are often focused on a specific topic of immediate interest that has arisen in the context of an ongoing exchange. Finally, ethnographic interviews often take place over time, enabling the researcher to follow up with the participants as needed to expand the understanding developed from earlier contacts.

Ethnographic interviews need to consider the declared state of the respondent and compare it to what appears to be their actual state. The researcher needs to avoid situations where there is considerable mismatch between the two states or the data collected may not be representative. Ethnographic interviewers also need to be careful in wording their questions so their participants can understand them. The memory of the participants can also be an issue. Participants may not be accurate in their recall of specifics about information and decisions. A final cautionary area is the reason or support for the interviews. Unless the researcher is careful, the supporting body or frame may have a bias on the way participants respond (Gobo, 2008).

Recommended Reading and References

Angrosino, M. V. (2007). Recontextualizing Observation: Ethnography, Pedagogy, and the Prospects for a Progressive Political Agenda. In N. K. Denzin & Y. S. Lincoln (Eds.), *The Sage Handbook of Qualitative Research*, 3rd ed. (pp. 729-746). Thousand Oaks, CA: Sage.

Atkinson, P. & Hammersley, M. (1994). Ethnography and Participant Observation. In N. K. Denzin & Y. S. Lincoln (Eds.), *Handbook of Qualitative Research* (pp. 248-261). Thousand Oaks, CA: Sage.

Fielding, N. G. (2006). Ethnographic Interviewing. In V. Jupp, *The Sage Dictionary of Social Research Methods*. London, England: Sage. doi: 10.4135/9780857020116

Gobo, G. (2008). *Doing Ethnography*. London, England: Sage Publications Ltd. doi: 10.4135/9780857028976

Rules of Thumb for Size of Qualitative Samples

Qualitative Studies

Sample size for qualitative studies depends upon your research question and purpose, instead of formal statistical rules like those used for quantitative studies. Some general rules have emerged in the literature to keep in mind.

For preliminary studies, class project studies, master's level studies:

One study containing three to six detailed analyses, plus detailed *microanalyses* exploring the similarities and differences between participants.

> *Sample size for qualitative studies depends upon your research question and purpose instead of on formal statistical rules.*

For Ph.D. dissertation studies:

Several self-contained but related studies designed to explore in—depth and triangulate the phenomenon of interest. One such set of related studies includes the following:

- Begin with a case study of a single representative participant analyzed carefully and in detail to develop an understanding of the phenomenon as it exists in the experiences and mind of the representative participant. This information can guide the development of interviewing questions and processes for additional participants.
- Move to detailed interviews and analyses of a representative sample of three to six participants. Analysis of the data from this study will confirm that the experiences of the participants map to the theoretical predictions, the phenomenon exists in a way that is amenable to qualitative analysis to discover underlying patterns, or the phenomenon is unknown but important to understand.
- Triangulation and confirmation of the findings from the two previous steps in a larger sample of eight or more participants, with the final

number determined either by theoretical considerations or data saturation (including failure to obtain data saturation).

For Professional Doctoral Dissertation Studies:

Because the focus of professional doctorates is more on in-depth understanding of specifics and less on generalizability, many professional doctoral programs accept studies structured to develop a deeper but less generalizable understanding of the phenomena of interest.

For professional doctoral studies, a common sample is four to ten participants who participate in two rounds of interviewing. The first interview collects information and serves as a stimulus preparing participants for the second interview. Analysis of the results from both rounds completes identification and mapping of the patterns and then extends that into comparisons and contrasts between participant experiences and the relevance of similarities and differences to understanding the phenomenon.

WORKSHEET 5.3: *Qualitative Research Checklist*

- ☐ Research was directed by a clear research question.
- ☐ Qualitative approach was carefully selected to answer research question and match environment.
- ☐ Study was carefully planned based on the assumptions of the approach selected.
- ☐ Researcher is knowledgeable about qualitative approaches and follows standard procedures.
- ☐ Research has a primary focus related to the problem and purpose for the study.
- ☐ Rigorous data collection and management procedures were followed.
- ☐ If more than one approach was used, research clearly differentiated approaches and described unique results from each perspective.
- ☐ Interpretive analysis was conducted at several levels of abstraction.
- ☐ Final report is clear and written to be engaging, presenting ideas and insights in a thoughtful and engaging way.

Recommended Reading and References

Creswell, J. W. (1998). *Qualitative Inquiry and Research Design: Choosing among Five Traditions.* Thousand Oaks, CA: Sage.

Stake, R. E. (2005). Qualitative case studies. In N. K. Denzin & Y. S. Lincoln (Eds.), The Sage Handbook of Qualitative Research, 3rd ed. (pp. 443-466). Thousand Oaks, CA: Sage.

Strauss, A. & Corbin, J. (1998). *Basics of Qualitative Research: Techniques and Procedures for Developing Grounded Theory.* Thousand Oaks, CA: Sage.

CHAPTER 6

Quantitative Research

Kelley A. Conrad, PhD

Experimental designs are the standard approach by researchers following the scientific method to study the effects of their independent variables on their dependent variables. The scientific method and associated designs are not unique to any given specialty. The scientific method has developed over the last couple of centuries as a method that generates results that will stand up to serious scrutiny. Because the pattern of the process is well known, it also provides a consistently rigorous routine for collecting and evaluating data.

The classic description of the scientific method is that it is composed of seven steps followed in the same order:

1. Identify a topic
2. Identify a research question
3. Design the study
4. Collect data
5. Analyze data
6. Interpret data, and
7. Inform others of the results.

Whether your interest is in answering a question posed by a friend or the need to complete a formal study like a dissertation, you can study it using the scientific method. Others will recognize your approach as systematic and attaches more value to your results than if you are less systematic.

Intervention designs are quantitative designs where the researcher wants to evaluate the effect of some intervention or treatment on a group; for example evaluating the effects of training or experience on participants exposed to the treatment in comparison to another group not receiving the treatment.

Recommended Reading and References

Campbell, D. & Stanley, J. (1963). Experimental and Quasi-Experimental Designs for Research. Chicago, IL: Rand McNally.

Kuhn, T. S. (1996). *The Structure of Scientific Revolutions* (3rd ed.). Chicago, IL: University of Chicago Press.

Quantitative Research

The research journey you have been traveling in this book now brings you to another world of investigation. A world where observations are transformed into data. The data can be simple named categories like sorting participants into groups that are named for a certain attribute. A common one is to compare groups by the gender of the members. There are many such groups, and sometimes the only information you have about a group of interest is the name it has. You might share the concern of many researchers that simply naming a group is not very sophisticated and you would be right. However, if that is all you have, then it is possible to do some comparative and correlational analyses based primarily on group membership. When you work with groups based on their identification by name, you have nominal data. Another way of thinking of nominal data is that each category represents a different state with those participants sharing the particular state having the same name applied to their group. Quite often, researchers begin with nominal data because we do not know much about what is going on and it is a convenient place to begin.

Usually, you have a bit more information. Perhaps you can order or rank the members of a group on some characteristic or attribute. When you can do this, you have ordinal data—that is, data that orders the participants in some way. There are many ways you can order your participants. These range from taking physical measurements (height, weight, age, etc.) to having the people complete some measure and ordering them based on the scores. This can be accomplished with virtually any test that is scored. We can now say more than people in the different groups are different, we can add the level of difference. Our participants who received higher scores have *more* of what ever was being measured. While this is a step toward better understanding, you have not gained a lot since knowing one individual has more of an attribute being measured does not tell you how much more of the attribute is present.

If you think it would be nice to know how much more, you are right, it is desireable for a researcher to know how much more of the attribute is present. To accomplish that, you move to the next more detailed and better level of measurement, interval measurement. With an interval scale, you have a ruler that has equal intervals defined so you can assess how much more or less of what you are measuring is present. This sounds simple and it is used when you think of physical measurement with a measuring stick like a ruler. What if you want to measure a psychological characteristic, say the amount of anxiety a student felt when anticipating a test? We could assess this with scale developed working with students, which could then be used to measure their level of anxiety. Similar psychological scales are developed all the time. If you have one, can you say that the difference between two identical score pairs on your scale is the same for all participants who used the scale? That is right, you can not. Rating scales appear to provide real interval data, but often do not. So what are you to do?

The best scales to use in research are known as ratio scales. They are scales with an absolute zero. How does that help? If a student on our text anxiety scale had absolutely no anxiety, that student would score zero on the scale. Combined with equal intervals, the absolute zero condition makes your measurement scale a ratio scale. This sounds great but is very hard to achieve. Some psychologists use magnitude estimation where participants are given a reference point and then asked to use that as the base for their rating. For example, a student could be told that average test anxiety felt by college students is 50 and then is asked to estimate what percentage of the average anxiety he or she feels. If they felt twice as anxious, they would report a level of 100. Magnitude estimation is about as good as a psychological scale gets.

Why is all this important? The scale of measurement you have directly influences the analyses you can perform. This, in turn, is directly related to the research question you are asking. Ask yourself, "What scale of measurement do I need to answer my research question? What measures can I find or create that will provide the level of measurement I need?"

Return to Your Research Journey

In the previous chapter, you saw how the stair steps to success moved your research journey forward. You were able to see qualitative research as a disciplined approach connected to the scientific method. In a similar fashion, a "parallel stair steps" model illustrates how each phase of a quantitative analysis builds on the previous ones and provides an overview of quantitative analysis.

Quantitative Analysis—Stair Steps to Success

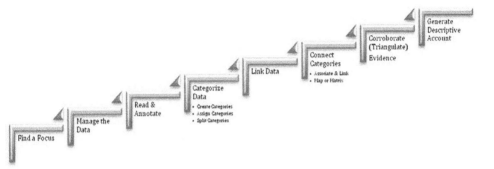

Focusing

Your research focus for a quantitative study is similar to what you might have for a qualitative study. The main difference is that you have selected a way of measuring your results that will be quantitative and based on some numerical scaling. Most quantiative studies follow earlier studies that validated an instrument or theory that can be tested.

Designing

For quantitative studies, the experimental design becomes a critical component. It is your design that allows you to conclude that the factors in which you are interested have the effect you are reporting. To accomplish this result, you need to select two identical groups or two matched groups and treat them alike, except for your experimental treatment. Your experimental design describes how you control the situation to make your deductions as accurate as possible. There are many ways your study can be affected by variables other than the one you are interested in. Good design helps you increase the internal validity of your study by controlling for selection, maturation, regression, attrition, interactions, history, testing, and instrumentation (Campbell & Stanley, 1963). When done carefully, your design keeps you from making incorrect deductions and inferences.

Measuring

Your measures need to have two attributes. They need to really measure the construct you are interested in. That is, they have *content validity*. Sometimes know as content sampling, this means the measure includes all aspects of interest from the content area and is a large enough sample to be accurate. The other attribute is *reliability*. A measure is reliable when it produces consistent results. A common way to check reliability is to use the measure twice and see if the test retest results are the same.

Sampling

You seldom have the resources or funds needed to measure all the members of your population of interest. Because of this, you need to use an accessible group of participants you can measure as a stand-in for the population. How you select or sample these participants is important and will affect your results. There are two major strategies: non*probability sampling*, which you use when random sampling is impossible, and probability sampling, which is structured so all members of a population have an equal opportunity to be included.

Collecting

You might think data collection is a no brainer. Simply send out your instrument and have people send in their results. Unfortunately, many factors can affect the data you collect, so being thoughtful, disciplined, and systematic are important. Collection begins with the instructions given to your participants, the wording and ordering of the questions, the entry of the results, the processing of the data, the cleaning of the data, and ends with the reduction and summary of the data.

Analyzing

Analysis is both simple and complex. It is simple in that all your analyses begin with the basic comparison derived from the logic of the scientific method. You have a population of interest and a sample from that population who have agreed to participate. You will randomly divide your sample into two independent similar groups. One group you will treat by giving them your experimental treatment, and the other group you will leave alone while controlling all other factors. The basic analysis is to compare the results for the two groups. To do this, you compute the means while controlling for random effects (error) in your analysis. The t-test statistic is the generally accepted way of deciding if the differences found are big enough to be meaningful. As a researcher, you select how willing you are to be wrong based on your research question and the *risks of answering it incorrectly. For social science research*, you will often use risk levels of 1 chance in 100 ($p \leq .01$) or of 5 chances in 100 ($p \leq .05$).

Evaluating

Your biggest challenge will come toward the end. Few studies have clear-cut unambiguous results. You will study your data and interpret the findings for your readers. It is seldom sufficient to leave the interpretation solely to your readers. You also need to revisit your problem and hypotheses and explain to your readers how the results relate to your starting point and what are the conclusions to be made from that.

Reporting

Most studies are written up for publication or presentation. Your final report needs to cover the original research question and hypotheses, summarize the results, evaluate the hypotheses, interpret the results, discuss alternative interpretations, and explain problems and unexpected results. It is also customary to recommend future research and to discuss the practical applications of the work.

If your review of your problem statement and purpose statement brought you the conclusion that you will have data that can be measured and described using numbers, your method will be a quantitative one. Before you can select the appropriate method, you need to convert your research question or questions into research hypotheses. A research hypothesis is a testable prediction about the relationship between two or more variables in your study.

Converting a Research Question into Research Hypotheses

> *A research hypothesis states a direct, testable prediction about the relationship between two or more variables.*

Hypotheses are the direct statements of what you will test with your research. Many state the relationship you expect between two groups or two variables. The predictions of the relationships you make for the variables in your study when formalized in your design, become the hypotheses you will test. To be testable, a prediction about a hypothesis has to be tested as being right or wrong. Doing this successfully requires careful thought about the variables studied and their relationships. Key considerations for hypotheses are to make them theoretically based, testable, supportable, and relevant.

Theoretically Based Hypotheses

Connect your hypotheses to a theory and show how the hypotheses are related to the theoretical concepts and predictions. Theories make predictions that are good candidates for experimental tests. Some theories may be indirectly related to your topic but still provide support for your research. Gaps in the literature can be found by examining existing data for theoretically predicted outcomes.

For example, let's say you are interested in Festinger's (1957) cognitive dissonance theory. The theory predicts that when people have one belief, behaving inconsistently with that belief will bother them, and this is unpleasant for the person. In the words of the theory, they feel dissonance. The theory also predicts that because of the unpleasant feeling, a person experiencing dissonance will seek to reduce it by changing their thoughts or their behavior.

Let's say that when you started work on your dissertation you were confident of your knowledge and abilities and expected completing the process would be consistent with your experiences in your graduate level courses. However, let us say you have just received a scathing review of your proposal from your advisor. This review creates cognitive dissonance for you. While part of you is still confident about being successful, another part is devastated by the criticism and may be doubtful that you can be successful. In this dissonant state, cognitive dissonance theory predicts that you will take some kind of action either in thought or deed to reduce or eliminate the disparity. What might you do? You could drop out of the program. That decision might create further dissonance since you would be left with the lingering feeling you really could have succeeded. A second choice might be to meet with your advisor and review your work in order to understand how you were off the mark so you can make adjustments to do better in the future. This approach would reduce your dissonance and could be confirmed in the feedback on the next draft of your proposal.

To study your dissonance in the situations just described, you would need some way (perhaps a questionnaire on dissertation completion confidence) to assess your confidence of success before and after the review and the revision. Hypotheses are customarily stated as null hypotheses. Your null hypotheses for this study of your cognitive dissonance could be there will be no change in your measured confidence in your success as a dissertation student after the review from your advisor. Since there is a second measurement, you would add a second similar hypothesis: There will be no change in your measure confidence in your success as a dissertation student after the review by your advisor, following your revision of your proposal.

Your hypotheses are tested by evaluating the measurements and comparing your assessed confidence before and feedback with that of your confidence after each of the two postfeedback measures. If you find significant differences, you reject the hypotheses and accept the alternatives. Since the alternatives predict there will be significant differences and this prediction is consistent with cognitive dissonance theory, your research could be cited as supporting the theory.

Testable Hypotheses

State the relationships and outcomes you expect as clearly and simply as possible. A well-written hypothesis sets up the comparison you want to examine. This comparison drives the way you structure your design to create the comparisons and the statistical tests you can use to test the significance of the comparisons. Statistics are valuable as short hand ways to summarize how meaningful a particular comparison is, taking into consideration the characteristics of the sample and influences on the experiment. For example, say you are comparing the performance scores of two groups of students where one group (experimental group) experienced a special DVD (independent variable) in their class and one group (control group) did not. Knowing how much the two classes differ does not tell you the strength of the effect of the DVD. In fact, it is quite likely that even without using the DVD as a treatment, there would be some differences between the group scores. This could be due to random factors or some extraneous variable. Inferential statistics allows you to examine any difference you find against what you might expect to have purely by chance. When you say a difference is *statistically significant*, you are saying you used inferential statistics and have demonstrated that beyond some level of reasonable doubt (for social sciences this is typically the $p=.01$ or $p=.05$ level) you are confident the difference you found was not happenstance. Your probability level states your willingness to be wrong. For $p=.05$, you are willing to be wrong 5 times out of 100. For $p=.01$, you are willing to be wrong only 1 time in 100. How you decide which level to use depends on the costs and importance of being wrong. For most social science research, the p values of .05 and .01 are sufficiently accurate because most of our assessment instruments are not particularly precise. However, in medicine and other studies where the costs of an error are high (someone might die from taking a particular drug), the p values are much smaller to reflect the amount of acceptable risk. If we want the chance that only one person in million will die from the treatment, we would set our p value at .000001. To achieve this, we would need a very large sample and accurate measurement.

> *A well-written hypothesis sets up the comparison you want to examine.*

Supportable Hypotheses

The traditional way of stating hypotheses is to state the expected outcome and, when relevant, the direction it will take. It is customary to test hypotheses using statistics. This is because there are a number of statistical conventions that help other researchers quickly evaluate the importance of your findings. Statistically, it is the null hypotheses (that there is no relationship between the independent and dependent variables) that is tested and reported.

Null Hypotheses

A null hypothesis predicts no relationship between two variables. Be cautious of a common error, proving the null hypotheses by accepting it. You can only reject the null. When you do that, you can say you found a *treatment* effect. When you can't reject the null, you say you failed to find a treatment effect.

In our study of cognitive dissonance associated with dissertation proposal feedback, our null hypothesis derived from the theory is that there will be no dissonance (that is no effect). The treatment in this study is the feedback received from the advisor. After we assess the scores on the dissertation confidence measure, if what we find do not have significant differences between the scores prior to the feedback and those after the feedback, we cannot reject the null hypothesis (that there will not be a difference). Such results are sometimes called *null results*. This is a good term since such results are inconclusive. They could be caused by other factors like lack of power (not including enough participants in the sample) to correctly reject it (also known as a Type II error) or biased sampling, or some extraneous variable (error). To phrase that differently, you failed to discover a relationship between your measured dissertation confidence scores and the feedback even though one really exists.

> A *null hypothesis predicts no statistically significant relationship between two variables.*

WORKSHEET 6.1: My Hypotheses Worksheet

State the hypotheses for your quantitative dissertation:

Null Hypothesis:

Alternative Hypothesis:

More than one Null Hypothesis? Add them as needed.

Examine your hypotheses using the items below:

Provability
Can the hypotheses be proven wrong? (Are they operationalized and   Y / N
specific?)

Supportability
Do your hypotheses predict effects or relationships?   Y / N

Testability
Are your hypotheses logical and consistent with previous research   Y / N
and theory?

Relevancy
Are your hypotheses meaningful and relevant?   Y / N
(Consider theoretical predictions, previous research, and practical
applications)

Approvals
Can your study be conducted within the constraints of the requirements   Y / N
to protect human participants and protected classes?

Does it meet the institution's IRB requirements?   Y / N

Has your committee and chair given approval?   Y / N

Resources
Have you guaranteed you will have access to your participants?   Y / N

Do you have the physical resources to conduct your study?   Y / N

Have you estimated the costs and planned for them?   Y / N

List any questions or issues you need to resolve before proceeding with your study:

Experimental Method

Population

Most doctoral research in the social sciences studies people. The entire group of people who are of interest is the *population* for the study. Sometimes referred to as the *target population*, it is also the group to which you hope to be able to generalize the results of your study. Because of this, your description of the population needs to be detailed and specific. Typical details include age, gender, race/ethnicity, location, and other special defining characteristics.

When your group of interest is small, it may be possible to study all of the individuals. This type of study is called a *census study*, but is rare. Typically, the population is a much larger group than cannot be studied entirely. For this reason, you as the researcher, must select a subgroup from the population as a stand-in. This smaller group is known as the *research sample*. How the sample is selected and the accuracy with which it represents the population it is selected from is critical to your ability to generalize the results of the experiment.

Recommended Reading and References

Booth, W. C., Colomb, G. G. & Williams, J. M. (2003). *The Craft of Research* (2nd ed.). Chicago, IL, University of Chicago Press.

Kuhn, T. S. (1996). *The Structure of Scientific Revolutions* (3rd ed.). Chicago, IL: University of Chicago Press.

> *The target population is the group to which you hope to be able to generalize the results of your study.*

WORKSHEET 6.2: *My Dissertation Population Description*

Description of the largest group of people to which I would like the results of my study to apply:

General identification:

Age of participants (If an important and a defining characteristic for the study):

Gender of participants (If an important and a defining characteristic for the study):

Race or ethnicity of participants (If an important and a defining characteristic for the study):

Geographical location (If an important and a defining characteristic for the study):

Other characteristics defining the unique yet general characteristics of the group to which I want my study to apply:

Final Narrative Description of Target Population of Interest

This is one or two sentences or a short paragraph if complicated. It should be a full description, precise enough that someone wanting to duplicate or apply your study could select the same population.

Sampling

Since it is often inconvenient or impossible for you to complete census studies, you may select smaller groups to study. These smaller groups are *research samples*. Several strategies have been developed for the selection of samples so the individuals included will accurately represent the population from which they are drawn. There are two major approaches to sample selection: probabilistic sampling and nonprobabilistic sampling.

> *Research samples are smaller groups selected from the population of interest for convenience and economy.*

Probabilistic Sampling

You will use certain standard procedures to select probabilistic samples of individuals from the population in the most accurate, unbiased, and representative ways. There are four popular ways of selecting probabilistic samples:

Simple Random Sampling

Using this strategy, you select individuals for the sample so every individual in the population has an equal chance of being selected. A random sample can easily be created by assigning all individuals in the population a number and then using a random number table or generator to select the individuals to include.

Systematic Sampling

For systematic sampling, you select an interval and then simply select every participant on the list using that interval. For example, you might select every fifth individual from the list of people in the target population. Systematic samples are not quite as accurate as random samples in the way they represent the population from which they are selected, but systematic samples can be more convenient to select.

Stratified Sampling

You use stratified sampling when it is desired to make sure certain characteristics of the target population are represented in the study. For example, this would be important if your study was examining gender differences. To select a stratified sample, you would determine the percentages of the target population that are male and female. You would select a stratified sample by choosing a random sample from each gender until the percentage included in the experimental sample matches that of the target population. The sample would then be correctly stratified so the same percentage of males and females is in the sample as exists in the target population.

Multistage Cluster Sampling

When the target population is very large and you cannot obtain detailed demographics needed for stratifying, an alternative is to select random samples from representative subgroups. If you are interested in generalizing your results for all university and college graduates in the United States (a population for which it would be challenging, if not impossible, to develop a complete list), you could select random samples from various geographic regions or various types of universities (depending on which you want to include in your generalizations from your study). For example, say you were interested in college and university graduates from land grant institutions in the Midwest, you would develop a list of all land grant institutions in the Midwest and randomly select the ones to include in your study. Next, you would randomly select your participants from students at those colleges.

Recommended Reading and References

Blaikie, N. (2003). *Inferential Analysis: From Sample to Population. Analyzing Quantitative Data.* London, England: Sage Publications, Ltd. doi:10.4135/9781849208604

Frankfort-Nachmias, C. & Leon-Guerrero, A. (1997). *Social Statistics for a Diverse Society.* Thousand Oaks, CA: Pine Forge Press.

Henry, G. T. (1990). *Practical Sampling.* Thousand Oaks, CA: Sage. doi:10.4135/9781412985451

Kalton, G. (1983). *Introduction to Survey Sampling.* Newbury Park, CA: Sage.

Kish, L. (1965). *Survey Sampling.* New York, NY: Wiley

Wooldridge, J. M. (2008). Probabilistic Sampling. In T. Rudas (Ed.), *Handbook of Probability: Theory and Applications* (pp. 187-204). Thousand Oaks, CA: SAGE Publications, Inc.

Scherbaum, C. A. & Ferreter, J. M. (2009, April). Estimating Statistical Power and Required Sample Sizes for Organizational Research Using Multilevel Modeling. *Organizational Research Methods, 12*(2), (pp. 347-367). doi:10.1177/1094428107308906

Sudman, S. (1983). Applied Sampling. In P. H. Rossi, J. D. Wright, & A. B. Anderson (Eds.), *Handbook of Survey Research* (pp. 145-194). New York, NY: Academic Press.

Nonprobabilistic Sampling

Unfortunately, it is not always possible to use the rigorous requirements of probabilistic sampling when selecting the participants for a study. Sometimes, researchers decide to use individuals who are readily available. This can happen for a variety of reasons. The best of these reasons include that the researcher is specifically interested in a small group with special characteristics. Another reason is that the study will use volunteers or only individuals who consent to being studied. Nonprobabilistic samples are risky to use because the data collected only represents the group on which it was collected. While the results may do a good job of that, the researcher is usually interested in generalizing, and it cannot be easily done because the participants were not selected to be representative of a larger population.

Convenience Sampling

When a researcher uses participants who are handy primarily because they are available, the sampling approach is called convenience sampling. Common examples include using college students for subjects, using students in a school or class, using volunteers, and using self-selected volunteers who fill out an Internet-based survey.

Snowball Sampling

Originally developed for qualitative studies of highly specialized populations, snowball sampling asks participants to recommend others who share the characteristic to join in the study. For example, snowball sampling has been used for studies about drug users, homeless people, and gays. Snowball sampling can also be used to recruit participants using an organizational hierarchy. For example, a plant manager could be asked to send copies to all the supervisors who report to them, a principal to send copies to the teachers in their school, and a military leader to send copies to their direct subordinates.

Caution

While there are many times when nonprobabilstic sampling is perfectly acceptable, when a researcher chooses such an approach, it limits the generalization that is acceptable. A common error that a skilled researcher will avoid is overgeneralizing results from a convenience sample.

Recommended Reading and References

Henry, G. T. (1990). *Practical Sampling*. Thousand Oaks, CA: Sage Publications, Inc.

Thomas, S. L. (2006). Sampling: Rationale and Rigor in Choosing What to Observe. In Conrad, C. F. & Serlin, R. C. (Eds.), *The SAGE Handbook for Research in Education*. Thousand Oaks: SAGE Publications, Inc.

Conrad, Clifton F., and Serlin, Ronald C., 2006. "Sampling: Rationale and Rigor in Choosing What to Observe". The SAGE Handbook for Research in Education. Eds.Clifton F. Conrad, and Ronald C. Serlin. Thousand Oaks: SAGE Publications, Inc., 2006. March 14, 2012.

Conrad, Clifton F., and Serlin, Ronald C., 2006. "Sampling: Rationale and Rigor in Choosing What to Observe". In The SAGE Handbook for Research in Education, Eds.Clifton F. Conrad, and Ronald C. SerlinThousand Oaks: SAGE Publications, Inc. http://www.srmo.sagepub.com.ezproxy.apollolibrary.com/ view/the-sage-handbook-for-research-in-education/n22.xml

Conrad, C. F., and Serlin, R. C., 2006. Sampling: Rationale and Rigor in Choosing What to Observe. In: Conrad, C. F., and Serlin, R. C., eds.2006. The SAGE Handbook for Research in Education. Thousand Oaks: SAGE Publications, Inc. Available at: http://www.srmo.sagepub.com.ezproxy.apollolibrary.com/view/ the-sage-handbook-for-research-in-education/n22.xml [Accessed 14 March 2012]

WORKSHEET 6.3: Nonprobabilistic Sample

My rationale for basing my research on a nonprobabilistic sample:

What nonprobabilistic (convenience) strategy do I plan on using?

Why does that strategy make sense for my study?

Can I accept the limitations on generalizability using this sample imposes? Yes No

If yes, describe how you expect your results to be applied and interpreted.

If no, identify a way to select appropriate participants using a probabilistic approach that will allow you to generalize:

Write the description of your sampling method and your planned research sample for your method section:

Quantitative Studies

The preferred quantitative approach for determining the number of participants is to calculate the sample size needed for significant results.

You can calculate the exact sample sizes needed based on the statistics you will use to test the results. Using your test statistic, the desired level of probability, the number of variables, and the range of acceptable error, you can calculate the exact numbers of participants needed. These computations are known as power calculations. You need the following information for these calculations:

My desired level of statistical significance: $p = .05$ $p = .01$ Other?

My desired power (probability of correctly rejecting the null hypotheses): is typically .80.

My expected effect size (based on similar studies in the literature): typically set at .5

For each of the three parameters above, you should have a reason supporting your choice. Why is your desired level of statistical significance appropriate for your study?

How much risk can you accept in your study that you have made the wrong decision? Why is that risk acceptable to you and why should it be acceptable to those reading your study? (This is the flip side of power.)

A convenient calculator using the GPower formula is on the internet at:

http://www.psycho.uni-dusseldorf.de/aap/projects/gpower/

My calculated sample size to achieve desired statistical power (Provide all the entries in the GPower formula so if someone wanted to check your calculations, they could do so.)

General Rules of Thumb for Quantitative Studies

Minimum sample size for experimental studies should be about fifteen participants.

Minimum sample size for correlational studies of relationships is about thirty participants.

Minimum sample size for surveys varies by structure of survey, but about three hundred participants is an estimate. The more categories you plan to use in your analysis, the more participants you will need to reach significance.

WORKSHEET 6.4: My Dissertation Sampling

My target population is:

Types of individuals (Specify the group I want to talk about in my results and conclusions):

From what specific location (Specify the group I have access to or can conveniently visit. I have selected a group I can be reasonably sure of having access to for the duration of my study.):

With what specific characteristics (Those characteristics critically important to my study):

Is it feasible to complete a census study (Include the entire population in my study? This may be possible and wise if the population of interest is limited to a small number of individuals. For example, all the students in a class, all the patients in a clinic, and all the supervisors in a company.)

If not, which sampling method can I use to obtain the most accurate, unbiased group representative of my target population?

Random Sampling
Systematic Sampling
Stratified Sampling
Multistage Cluster Sampling

Describe the strategy for selecting the sample I will use: (Be specific enough here that another researcher could replicate your study by selecting a sample that would be highly similar in characteristics to the one you selected.)

Why is this strategy the best one to use for my study? (Here, it is important to describe the logic supporting why the strategy makes sense for your study.)

Types of Experimental Designs

After the Fact Designs

After the fact, designs are also called ex post facto studies. You would choose such a design when you notice that something unusual has happened and are wondering *after the fact* what could have caused that effect. You are reasoning backwards from the effect to what might have been an influence or the cause. These designs are sometimes called preexperimental designs because they often lead directly to experimental studies of the same problem.

Because after the fact designs are posttest-only studies, they are not powerful and should be avoided when generalization is desired.

A posttest-only design is only descriptive. You might use it after treatment or training when it is impossible to obtain a premeasure. The results are difficult to interpret since only one measure is available and the usual controls for variables affecting the outcomes are missing.

The pretest/posttest design is an improvement on the posttest-only design in that it reduces the possibility that the final performance is a function of capabilities that existed prior to the treatment or training. However, because there is no control group, you cannot rule out the influence of some other intervening factor as the cause for the effect.

Experimental Designs

Experimental designs compare pretest and posttest changes for experimental and control groups. This structure enables you to determine whether changes are due to the variations of independent variable.

Experimental designs add a control group in which you give the same measures pre—and posttreatment to an experimental and a control group. In place of the treatment or training

> *You choose an ex-post facto study when you notice something has happened and you are wondering after the fact what could have been an influence or cause.*

being evaluated in the experimental group, the control group engages in some other activity.

A more sophisticated experimental design, the Solomon four-group design (Solomon, 1949), has one experimental and three control groups. Using this design, you can evaluate the pretest as if it were a treatment as well as the experimental manipulation of the independent variable. This

> *Experimental designs compare pre-test and post-test changes for experimental and control groups.*

design allows you to evaluate and control of any testing effect resulting from the pretests.

In the next few pages we will explore six major designs: Posttest Only, Two Groups Posttest, Control Group, Solomon Four-Group, Nonequivalent Control, and Time Series.

Quasi-Experimental Designs

In many naturally occurring social and work situations of interest, it is not possible to exert the control needed for experimental designs. Partial control may exist because of existing groups or classifications.

Time series designs capitalize on situations where there is regular ongoing assessment. It is possible to insert training or treatment between two such regularly scheduled measurements and examine the impact of the assessments that follow that intervention.

In nonequivalent control groups, a different but similar group is selected for the control group. This is useful when it is impossible to select both experimental and control groups from one area of an organization.

Recommended Reading and References

Andranovich, G. D. & Riposa, G., (1993). *Research Design. Doing Urban Research.* Thousand Oaks, CA: SAGE. doi: 10.4135/9781412983983

Darius, P. & Portier, K. (1999). Experimental Design. In Ader, H. J. & Mellenbergh, G. J. (Eds.), *Research Methodology in Social Behavioural and Life Sciences* (pp. 67-95). London, England: Sage Publications, Ltd.

Solomon Four-Group Design. (2012, March). *The SAGE Encyclopedia of Social Science Research Methods.* Retrieved from http://www.srmo.sagepub.com

Solomon, R. L. (1949). An Extension of Control Group Design. *Psychological Bulletin, 46,* 137-150.

Posttest-Only Quantitative Designs

Although the posttest-only design does not fit the traditional requirements for an experimental design, it can be used when the researcher controls for problems of internal invalidity and for any interaction between the posttest and the treatment (Campbell & Stanley, 1963).

Posttest-only designs can be helpful in situations where the research is assured of random assignment to the treatment and control groups, but cannot obtain a pretest assessment.

Many designs are diagrammed using a shorthand developed by Campbell and Stanley (1963) in their classic book on experimental designs.

Symbols used in the design maps are as follows:

R = Random selection
N = Nonrandom selection
X = Experimental treatment or stimulus being evaluated—the independent variable
O = Observations or tests of effects
—= No activity or neutral activity

The pattern for the posttest-only design is:

R—X O

Read this as randomly selected participants, no activity, treatment, ending with observation (Posttest).

A second variation of the posttest-only design compares scores on the posttest for the group receiving the treatment to a second randomly selected group, which did not receive the treatment. This version is closer to an experimental design and when the assignment of participants is truly random, it should produce similar results. The pattern for this design is:

R __ X O
R __ __ O

Recommended Reading and References

Campbell, D. & Stanley, J. (1963). *Experimental and Quasi-Experimental Designs for Research*. Chicago, IL: Rand McNally.

WORKSHEET 6.4: Posttest-Only Design

Use this checklist to remind yourself of the important elements that need to be considered in your design if it is to accomplish the objectives of your study.

To use a posttest-only design effectively:

☐ Randomly assign participants to the experimental and control groups. (This is critical!)
(Random assignment is what satisfies the requirement for groups to be equal.)
☐ Your participants will then be comparable to the dependent variable at the beginning of your study.
(Usually they are similar enough to satisfy most statistical tests.)
☐ When you use the first model, you cannot statistically test the results.
☐ When you use the second model, you can use a t-test to compare the treatment group to the randomly selected nontreatment group.
(When done carefully, this two-group approach can be as powerful and effective as the traditional two-group, pre—and posttest classic experiment)
☐ With the two-group, posttest-only model, you can compare the posttest scores for significant differences using a t-test.

Pre—and Posttest Control Quantitative Design

> The pretest-posttest control group design is the classical pure experimental design.

The pretest-posttest control group design is the classical pure experimental design. This design formed the basis of most of the formal research in science before the 1970s and remains one of the most popular designs today. It is very similar to the posttest-only design and simply adds a pretest to each group. This addition enables the researcher to check that the two groups are equivalent on the pretest measure, but it also adds the complication of possible test effects. These occur when, by virtue of taking the test once, participants learn something about it that enhances their scores on the posttest independently of what the effect of the treatment might be.

The pattern for the pre—and posttest design using two groups is

    R O X O
    R O—O

The correct statistical test is the t-test for the difference between the two posttest scores.

A popular version of the pre—and posttest design is the Solomon Four-Group design. This design adds the posttest-only, two-group design to the pretest-posttest control group design, creating four groups of participants such that every combination of pretest, treatment, and posttest is experienced by one group of participants. This design is popular when there are concerns about the potential influence of the pretests on the posttest results. The model for this design is:

    R O X O
    R O—O
    R __ X O
    R __ __ O

Recommended Reading and References

Babbie, E., (2010). *The Practice of Social Research* (12th ed.). Belmont, CA: Wadsworth.

Campbell, D. & Stanley, J. (1963). *Experimental and Quasi-Experimental Designs for Research*. Chicago, IL: Rand McNally.

Huck, S. W. & Sandler, H. M. (1973). A Note on the Solomon Four-Group Design: Appropriate Statistical Analysis. *The Journal of Experimental Education, 42*, 54-55.

Solomon, R. L. (1949). An Extension of Control Group Design. *Psychological Bulletin, 46*, 137-150.

Trochim, W. (2000). *The Research Methods Knowledge Base* (2nd ed.). Cincinnati, OH: Atomic Dog Publishing.

Van Engelenburg, G. (1999). *Statistical Analysis for the Solomon Four-Group Design.* [Research report pp. 99-06]. Faculty of Educational Science and Technology, University of Twente: The Netherlands.

Walton-Braver, M. C. & Braver, S. L. (1988). A Meta-Analysis of Pretest Sensitization Effects in Experimental Design. *American Educational Research Journal, 19,* 249-258.

WORKSHEET 6.5: Pre- and Posttest Design

Use this checklist to remind yourself of the important elements that need to be considered in your design if it is to accomplish the objectives of your study.

- ☐ I selected two identical groups and checked that they were normally distributed and had the same scores on the pretest.
- ☐ I treated the groups identically except for the treatment (experimental group).
- ☐ My final comparison between the posttest results for the treatment to the posttest results for the control group.
- ☐ I controlled for self-selection bias by using random selection.
- ☐ I checked for maturation bias.
- ☐ I checked for attrition that might have affected my results.
- ☐ I have checked for extreme, outlying scores and regression toward the mean.
- ☐ I reviewed the history of the environment for any major changes that might have affected participants.
- ☐ I evaluated my data for any measurement effects that might have distorted my results.
- ☐ I made sure there were no changes between pre—and posttest administration of the measures.
- ☐ I made no changes in the instruments used for measurement.

Quasi-Experimental Quantitative Designs

In some circumstances, we cannot randomly assign our participants without creating disruption to the area or variables we want to study. However, in some situations we can identify two groups that we can assume should be equivalent at the beginning of the study but had different experiences, which we can assess with postexperience measures. Probably, the most frequently used quasi-experimental design is the nonequivalent groups design. In this design, we identify two similar but different groups, for example, two classes at the same grade level in the same school. These are intact groups, but we did not select them randomly so there may be some factors affecting the participants included in those groups that we are not aware of. Nonetheless, we treat them as if they were equal. After identifying the groups, we move ahead as if this were true experiments. The model for this approach is:

> *The quasi-experimental design is used when we cannot randomly assign participants and when we can assume the comparison groups should be equivalent.*

    N O X O
    N O—O

Note, we changed the initial letter for our samples to N indicating these two groups are nonrandom.

As with the pure experimental design, our test statistic is still a t-test. However, we will want to test for a difference on the pretest as well as the posttest. This design can result in a number of different patterns between the pretest and posttest results. The nonrandom and possible nonequivalence of the two groups complicates the analysis and requires extra care during interpretation.

The final design we will discuss is the time series quasi-experimental design. Such designs use measurements that take over time, usually at regular intervals. The researcher tests and retests the same participants. Each earlier test can be considered a pretest for any of the later posttests. Some interesting new effects can be evaluated in time series designs. These are maturation effects, mortality effects, and regression effects. The biggest threat to this design is history. Many things can happen that affect the variables being measured as the time of the study is extended.

Recommended Reading and References

Campbell, D. & Stanley, J. (1963). *Experimental and Quasi-Experimental Designs for Research.* Chicago, IL: Rand McNally.

WORKSHEET 6.6: My Quasi-Experimental Design

Did I choose the most powerful quasi-experimental design I can use? If the regression-discontinuity design is appropriate, did I assign individuals to treatment and control groups solely on the basis of their cutoff score on the assignment variable?

How did I carefully select the cutoff score? Describe the considerations and the reasons for my selection.

What is the specific score I selected? Do I understand and can I explain the importance of this cutoff score to the analysis?

Did I select a time series design? If so, did I include a control series? Does the situation fit the requirements of an interrupted time series design? How? Are there enough data points in the series to allow me to estimate the error structure and complete a responsible analysis?

What are the dimensions of my analysis? What is the form of the effect, the permanance of the effect, and the immediacy of the effect?

Action Research—Designs with Intervention

Lewin (1948) is credited with the identification and naming of action research. He noted,

The research needed for social practice can best be characterized as research for social management or social engineering. It is a type of action research, a comparative research on the conditions and effects of various forms of social action, and research leading to social action. Research that produces nothing but books will not suffice. (pp. 202-203)

> *Action research is a practitioner-focused approach, essentially reflexive thought and intervention in ongoing professional practice.*

More recently, Bogdan and Biklen (1992) described action research as a frame of mind being, "a perspective that people take toward objects and activities" (p. 223). Today, there are two major schools of action research. One is closely attached to education and sees action research as,

simply a form of self-reflective enquiry undertaken by participants in social situations in order to improve the rationality and justice of their own practices, their understanding of these practices, and the situations in which the practices are carried out. (Carr & Kemmis, 1986, p. 162)

This is a practitioner-focused approach, essentially reflexive thought and intervention in ongoing professional practice.

The second school of thought about action research is commonly seen in analysis of social welfare interventions. Bogdan and Biklen (1992) described this tradition by noting,

its practitioners marshal evidence or data to expose unjust practices or environmental dangers and recommend actions for change . . . . [I]t is linked into traditions of citizen's action and community organizing. The practitioner is actively involved in the cause for which the research is conducted. For others, it is such commitment is a necessary part of being a practitioner or member of a community of practice. (p. 223)

Action research is different from professional practice or consulting and teaching because it uses the scientific approach. The researcher is systematic in approach and follows a cyclical strategy of diagnosing the problem; considering, selecting, and taking action; evaluating the consequences; and then specifying learning and modifying the approach (Susman, 1983). This pattern continues in a repeating cycle. Action research changes participants into researchers, takes place in real-world social situations, addresses real problems, and has researchers who do not attempt to be objective, but who freely acknowledge their bias to the other participants.

Winter (1989) advanced action research by providing a descriptive summary of the six key principles underlying the approach. These are:

Reflexive Critique—The forthright claims by the accounts to be authoritative. This is considered reflective since the people consider the issues and processes in order to state explicitly their interpretations and assumptions.

Dialectical Critique—The social dialogue about the research is the way the phenomena are conceptualized. Because of this, the dialogue is necessary. The focus is usually on elements that are unstable or in opposition, since that is usually where change will happen.

Collaborative Resource—Participants are coresearchers whose ideas are considered resources for significant ideas about the interpretation of the issues or processes.

Risk—Open discussions about interpretations, ideas, and judgments are risky. They open one to criticism. Action researchers make an effort to avoid such risk and reduce the impact by explaining to others that the researcher is a subject also.

Plural Structure—Action research entertains multiple perspectives and comments. These, in turn, lead to a variety of actions and interpretations. One of the richness of action research is the many varieties of accounts, explanations, and theories that can emerge and be reported.

Theory, Practice, Transformation—Winter (1989) summarized the distinguishing principle, "For action researchers, theory informs practice, practice refines theory, in a continuous transformation" (p. 44).

Types of Action Research

Traditional action research is often seen in work in organizations. It includes components from field theory, group dynamics, T-groups, and clinical models. Traditional action research is conservative and maintains the existing organizational power structures.

Contextual Action Research or Action Learning

Action learning is based on Trist's work investigating intra organizational relationships. It is contextual and endeavors to assess how individuals develop their understanding of the whole and how they use that understanding.

Radical Action Research

With roots in Marxism and praxis, radical action research focuses on emancipation and removing power imbalances. Radical action research is seen in feminist, liberationist, and international development groups.

Educational Action Research

This branch of action research is one of the most popular and is based on the writing of John Dewey. Educational action research views educators as involved in community problem solving and the application of learning in a social context.

Methods for Action Research

Action research uses a holistic approach and, as a consequence, applies different research methods as appropriate. Common tools include research journals, historical and current document collection, content analysis, participant observations, questionnaires, interviews, and case studies.

Recommended Reading and References

Atweh, B., Kemmis, S. & Weeks, P. (Eds.) (1998). *Action Research in Practice: Partnership for Social Justice in Education*. London, England: Routledge.

Bogdan, R. & Biklen, S. K. (1992). *Qualitative Research for Education*. Boston, MA: Allyn and Bacon.

Carr, W. & Kemmis, S. (1986). *Becoming Critical. Education, Knowledge and Action Research*. Lewes, England: Falmer.

Carson, T. R. & Sumara, D. J. (Eds.) (1997). *Action Research as a Living Practice*. New York, NY: Peter Lang.

Dadds, M. (1995). *Passionate Enquiry and School Development. A Story about Action Research*. London, England: Falmer.

Elliot, J. (1991). *Action Research for Educational Change*. Buckingham, England: Open University Press.

Ferrance, E. (2000). *Themes in Education: Action Research*. Providence, RI: LAB at Brown University, The Education Alliance.

Johnson, A. P. (2007). *A Short Guide to Action Research* (3rd ed.). New York, NY: Allyn and Bacon.

McNiff, J. (1993) *Teaching as Learning: An Action Research Approach.* London, England: Routledge.

McNiff, J., Whitehead, J. & Lomax, P. (2003). *You and Your Action Research Project.* London, England: Routledge.

O'Brien, R. (1998). *An Overview of the Methodological Approach of Action Research.* Toronto, Canada: University of Toronto.

Quigley, B. A. & Kuhne, G. W. (Eds.) (1997). *Creating Practical Knowledge through Action Research.* San Francisco, CA: Jossey Bass.

Stringer, E. T. (2007). *Action Research: A Handbook for Practitioners* (3rd ed.). Newbury Park, CA: Sage.

Whyte, W. F. (Ed.) (1991). *Participatory Action Research.* Newbury Park, CA: Sage.

Winter, R. (1989). *Learning from Experience: Principles and Practice in Action Research.* Philadelphia, PA: The Flamer Press.

WORKSHEET 6.7: Planning Action Research

What is my one meaningful question? One that can be accomplished within the confines of the situation I will be using. State this as an open-ended, concise, meaningful question, preferably something you have influence over.

What data will be the most meaningful to collect? How will I collect that data? Is the data quantifiable or will it need to be viewed holistically?

After reviewing the data, what kind of action is appropriate to take, based on the evidence on hand? How does that action relate to the current literature? What is my plan for implementing the action?

What were the results? What change occurred? Was it an improvement? Would others agree? What is my evidence?

What should I do to follow up? Are there more questions that need to be addressed? Can the situation be improved? How?

Statistical Analysis Decision Trees

Choosing the correct analysis for your study is a fairly simple process. However, picking up a statistical text and reading through it can make the process seem very daunting. The decision trees diagrammed in the pages that follow can help you make the right choice for your analysis by selecting one of two choices at various decision points based on what your problem and purpose are and the kind of data you have collected.

Begin with your research question. Does it ask about the relationships between variables, or does it ask about the differences between groups? Next, ask what kind of data you have. Is it high-quality data based on an interval or ratio scale, or is it more basic data that is either nominal or ordinal? These choices are illustrated in the figure below.

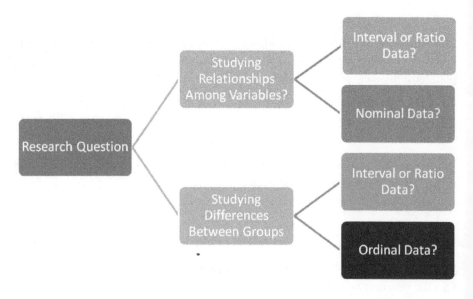

Each of the four answers on the right of the diagram above leads you to additional decision trees, each unique for the question and the type of scale used to collect your data.

Studying Relationships among Variables with Interval or Ratio Data

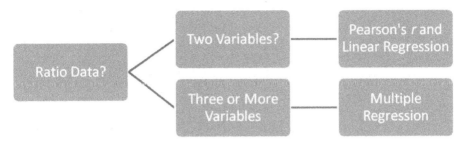

Studying Relationships among Variables with Ordinal Data

Studying Relationships among Variables with Nominal Data

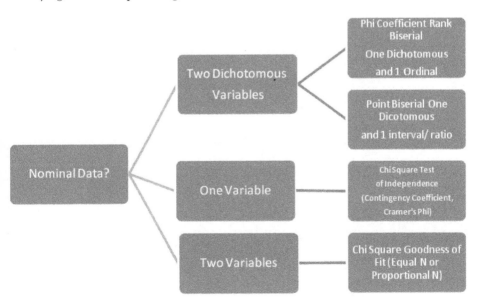

140 Quantitative Research

Studying Differences between Groups with Interval/Ratio Data

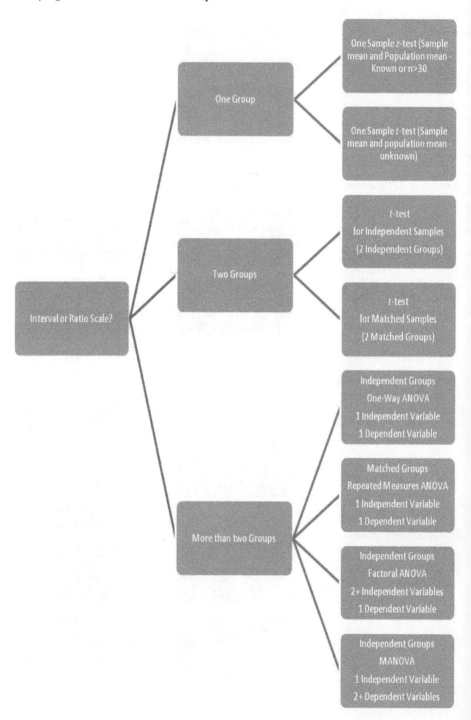

Studying Differences between Groups with Ordinal Data

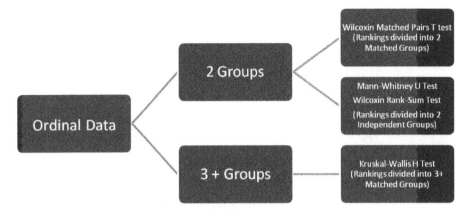

Did you find these flowcharts helpful making the decision about what statistical analysis was appropriate for your question and design? You should have been able to easily select the analysis appropriate for your problem, type of data, and method.

Conclusions and Recommendations

By the time you get through with your analysis, you will know your data and results better than anyone. Your final task in your journey is to communicate the results and the conclusions they lead you to in a clear and persuasive fashion so others can make good use of your work. Decide on your main conclusion, and the best place is to place it in your final chapter. You may want to make a big splash and present it at the beginning, or you may prefer to wait until the very end in order to leave people with a fresh perspective based on your research. The choice is yours.

Many people find outlining their thinking helps to keep it focused. Briefly describe the background including your original problem, purpose, hypotheses, and results. You want to keep this short since your readers have just read your report in detail and you only want to remind them of the road they have traveled. Next, think about the best order in which to present your evidence and outline it so it is persuasive and complete. Booth, Colomb, and Williams (2003) compared research to gold mining: you, "dig up a lot, pick out a little, discard the rest" (p. 200). Find the gold in your work and point it out clearly. When you are satisfied, try out your argument on a friend or acquaintance and see if they are persuaded. If so, congratulations, you have succeeded, and your research is ready to be published.

CHAPTER 7

Working Effectively with Your Dissertation Chair and Committee

Tiffany L. Tibbs, PhD

Introduction

My life, measured by graduate student standards, was good. I had a clear plan for my research project and a great dissertation chair. I had successfully completed my master's project, and I was ready to begin the dissertation process.

My academic world came crashing down when my chair told me she was leaving. She had been recruited to another highly respected university. I admired this person tremendously, respected her professional accomplishments, and appreciated the way she shared her wisdom and constructive criticism. She had a good track record for her own research productivity and had mentored several other students to successful completion. Her departure meant I had a choice; I could relocate to another university or switch my research focus and find another dissertation chair. Where in the world was I going to find a replacement for her?

The truth is there wasn't a replacement. And I knew it. There wasn't another faculty member that was doing the same type of research at the university. I was devastated. However, in the long run (and if you are doing a dissertation, you should develop good long-range vision), my career benefited by taking this detour and finding another dissertation chair, although I couldn't have predicted it at the time. Eventually, I found my way with a different chair, different research focus, and different committee to help me create a new path. This chapter is devoted to discussing the critical role the dissertation chair and committee members play in the development and successful completion of the dissertation process, and how students can effectively select and work with this important team.

The Role of the Dissertation Chair and Committee Members

The dissertation chair performs several important functions during the dissertation process and beyond. The chair is the *primary advisor* on the development of your study and the completion of your dissertation. Thus, expertise in the research topic, knowledge about research design and methodology, and understanding of the dissertation process is critical. The chair also serves as the *main leader and connection* between you and the rest of the committee. Finally, the dissertation chair is charged with *judging the quality* of your analysis, interpretation, and writing, which requires critical and thoughtful feedback.

Your other committee members serve as a team of people that will help to further strengthen your project, as consultants with different sets of skills and expertise. They are also responsible for ensuring the quality of the research. It is common for committee members to raise concerns and comments throughout the process, but ultimately, if there are disagreements, members will often (but not always) defer to the chair's recommendation. There are certainly political ramifications to your selection of committee members. For example, certain faculty may have different philosophical approaches and a history of heated disagreements; other faculty members may have a reputation for being a helpful advocate to students. You want to try to ensure that you have a committee that works well together and with you. You may not always like your chair or committee members or appreciate the multiple revisions they suggest, but ultimately, if you trust them and respect their judgment, your overall dissertation will benefit.

Your relationship with your dissertation chair (and to some extent, your committee members) requires a long-term commitment. Most dissertations take years (from concept development, to proposal, study execution, analysis, writing, and defense). In addition, these faculty members have knowledge and connections that will help you beyond the dissertation defense. They can help you investigate postdoctoral research positions, prepare and apply for jobs and promotions, support your career with recommendation letters, and connect you to colleagues across the country. Be respectful, work hard, and be diplomatic about these relationships as it can have an impact on your career, past the point of dissertation. See Chapter 10 for specific ideas about how your chair can help you in your life after the dissertation. But I am getting ahead of myself; first you have to identify and assemble your team.

Selecting a Mentor and Committee Members

If I could give you one piece of advice, I would say *choose your chair wisely*. Your chair has the potential to make your dissertation process either a great learning experience or a frustrating marathon that never seems to end. A good chair shares his or her expertise and wisdom, directs you to the resources you need, reviews questions and drafts thoughtfully and critically, and ultimately wants you to succeed. A good chair makes you work hard, but also encourages you to persevere. There are a lot of good chairs in academics, but there are also some mediocre ones, either because of lack of time, lack of knowledge, or lack of interest. And we have probably all heard war stories from those students who picked chairs who made the student's life a living hell. Choose wisely.

First, carefully consider what you want and need in a dissertation chair and committee members (see Worksheet 7.1 for a self-assessment checklist). No one person will meet all of your needs; however, in general, you should choose your dissertation chair based on content expertise, availability, and compatibility. One mistake some students make is to not think carefully about what they need in a chair; they hunt for a chair and hope to find them, or to take the first chair (or easiest faculty member or the only person that accepts them). This is a long-term investment, and this commitment should be taken seriously. Many students choose their graduate program, in part, because of the specific research program and dissertation chair available. Other students, because of the nature of the program, or norms and practices of the program, are encouraged to take classes and do projects first, before selecting a chair.

Make sure you *know what the university requirements are* so that you select faculty members who are *eligible* and appropriate. Universities and departments often have requirements about who can fulfill the role of dissertation chair and committee members (full-time faculty vs. adjunct; tenured vs. nontenured; length of time at university, number needed on the committee, etc.). Some departments have procedures for having *outside* readers for quality reviews, or extra members for the oral defense. Don't rely on potential chairs and committee members to know the specific requirements; educate yourself so that you only approach *eligible* faculty members, rather than wasting time on those who cannot fulfill the guidelines. Also, make sure you obtain all the correct forms for the formation of the committee and stages of the dissertation. Be prepared with the right forms and the right people at the right time.

Once you know what you need as a student, and what your department requires, *investigate who is available and who would be a good fit for you.* Use the right portion of Worksheet 7.1 to help you. Here are some strategies about how to find out about potential chairs:

- Do your homework. Learn about particular faculty members by reading their research publications and reviewing university information. Find out what resources they have to offer (research lab space, access to a participant population, national funding, and departmental connections). See how their past and current researches fit with your interests.
- Have an initial interview with this faculty member. Be polished and professional; they are evaluating you as a potential researcher and scholar, just

as you are evaluating them as a potential chair. Be ready to answer questions about your topic of interest, your potential plan for your dissertation, and how their research expertise fits that. Use this time to investigate key aspects of their content expertise, availability, and compatibility (see Worksheet 7.1 for more ideas).

- If you are already on-site, take a class, do a project (either as a volunteer or paid research assistant), or do your master's project with a particular faculty member to learn more about their style, type of research, guidance, and feedback. If you are in an online doctoral program, network among your peers to learn about faculty members whom you may want to approach to learn more about them and their research interests.
- Talk (but don't gossip) with other respected students or faculty members about their experience with this faculty member. Find out what perceived strengths (e.g., gives excellent written feedback) and weaknesses (e.g., is very busy, can only meet at certain times) this faculty member has, as well as recommendations for the best way to work with this person. Consider the source when weighing this information, as a struggling student may have more negative things to say.

Asking for Commitment and Setting Expectations

Once you have established what you need, what the department requires, and who you want to be your chair, it is time to make it official by asking the faculty member and setting expectations. *Set up a meeting with your potential chair to discuss your topic and the process of the dissertation.* For some, this is part of the interview and acceptance process of graduate school; for others, this occurs after they have been in the program, so adapt these suggestions accordingly. A few key items to remember when contacting your potential chair:

- Use a positive tone in your e-mail or phone message; let them know you appreciate their time (since most faculty members are very busy) to discuss the possibility of serving as your chairperson.
- Be clear about your status in the program, your potential dissertation topic, and why you think they would be a great dissertation chair.
- Request to talk (either face-to-face or by phone) about both the content of the dissertation proposal and the process/logistics of working together. If you are on-site, a face-to-face meeting is probably the best option; if you are in an online doctoral program, you could set up a phone call, Skype conference, or use other technology to have a personalized conversation.

- Ask if there is anything specific they would like to review before or at this meeting. It may be helpful to have an abstract, a one-page description of your topic ideas, or a list of questions to guide the meeting.
- Understand that most faculty members will want to discuss more about your topic and evaluate you as a student to determine if this is a good fit for them as well. Faculty members are, in part, evaluated by the quality, progress, and ultimate success of their dissertation mentees, so they want to choose wisely too!

In your meeting with your potential chair, you will want to *discuss the content of your dissertation.* Some of this may have been covered in an initial interview, but be ready to discuss in more depth your topic of interest, why it is important in the context of the broader research literature, and how it fits with the faculty member's research. Plan to discuss the method and design details for your potential study. Be prepared for them to have some challenging questions about your topic and design. Be ready to justify your choices, but also flexible enough to use their criticisms and concerns to think creatively how to adapt the project to make it stronger.

In addition to discussing the topic, it is important to discuss the process of dissertation development. You should *establish a clear, but flexible, dissertation work plan with expectations about communication, responsibilities, and timelines with your chair.* This consensual plan between the chair and the student sets the stage for clear expectations and open communication throughout the process. See Table 7a, and Worksheets 7.2 and 7.3) for worksheets to help you establish your dissertation work plan. Have these worksheets handy when meeting with your chair and committee members. Complete Table 7a to establish plans for communication, feedback, and expectations. Using some of the information discussed in Worksheet 7.2, then work with your chair to map out your specific dissertation tasks on a reasonable timeline in Worksheet 7.2. Finally, complete Worksheet 7.3 so that all members of the committee have key contact information for communication. Also see if the faculty member has any other guidelines they typically use or rules they suggest for dissertation students when establishing your dissertation work plan.

Once you have selected a dissertation chair and agreed upon your dissertation work plan, *talk with your chair about who should serve on your committee, based on your needs as a student and the qualities of your chair.* Aim to make your project as strong as possible by balancing out your committee in terms of expertise; consider strengths in methodology/design, statistical analysis, and knowledge of the study population. An equally important consideration is to make sure that your committee is relatively cohesive, so that you are not putting faculty members on the committee who historically have not gotten along. Ask your chair who they suggest, who they have worked with before, and who works well together. You don't want your proposal meetings or oral defense to be a setting for *turf battles* that have more to do with personality conflicts than the merit of your research. Have some ideas in mind about who you might suggest and why. Remember that you also need to fulfill university and department requirements for committee membership.

Once you and your chair have discussed topic, process, and committee membership, it is time to *invite the other faculty members to be part of your committee.* Apply similar strategies to your meetings or e-mail communications with potential committee members as you did with your chair. Indicate your interest and your chair's recommendation for them to serve on your committee. Review your proposed topic, potential study design, and dissertation work plan with them, and refine as needed. Keep your chair informed of these discussions, any additions to the dissertation work plan, and the finalized committee membership. Submit the appropriate signed forms to your department.

Note that some faculty members, due to timing, other responsibilities, or lack of fit (with topic or student personality) may decline your request to be your chair or on your committee. Do not take it personally. Be glad that this was established early in the process before significant time and investment occurred. Work with your chair or advisor to find appropriate replacements, and don't be discouraged.

Table 7a: Dissertation Work Plan: Communication, Feedback, and Expectations

Topic			
Communication			
Student provides progress updates and sends questions	*Method (e-mail, text, phone, in person)*	*How often?*	*Emergency procedure*
Student arranges key meetings	*What meetings are needed (key points in the process, proposal defense, oral defense, others)?*	*When?*	*Involving which members?*
Student sends drafts	*Basic guidelines for drafts (no grammar/ spelling mistakes, track changes or list documenting changes, others)?*	*When to send drafts, in order to provide enough review time for faculty (e.g., two weeks ahead of meeting date)?*	*Which members receive drafts? At which point in the process (rough drafts or final drafts)?*
Feedback			

Chair/committee member provides feedback on drafts	*What type (conceptual, editorial) and method (e-mail, phone, in person) of feedback will be provided?*	*How much time is typically needed for review (e.g., feedback will generally be returned within two weeks)?* *Are there certain periods when drafts are preferred (during semester/class) or times when chair/ member is not available to give feedback (summer, conferences)?*	*What to do if feedback is not received (e.g., if two weeks has passed, it is acceptable to send an e-mail prompt)?*
Student completes revisions based on feedback	*How to document revisions?*	*How much time is reasonable for revisions to be completed?*	*Who needs to review revisions?*
Expectations			
Expectations of chair/committee for student:			
Requests of student for chair/ committee:			

Working Together Effectively through the Process

Once you have assembled your team, it is time to begin proposal development. Based on your work plan, you will have outlined the input and roles of the chair and committee members during the different phases of the dissertation. One key piece of advice during the development of the proposal is to *meet early and often during the development of the proposal,* particularly with your chair. It is also advisable to have at least one meeting with the whole group so that everyone is on the same page about the direction of the research. This is the time to deal with questions and concerns, and to solve the problem together. It is critical to develop a well-designed study so that you have a strong project to defend. Some universities require a formal proposal defense and/or an outside review before moving forward with data collection.

Once your proposal is approved and you have IRB approval, you will also work closely with your chair, and depending on your work plan, and key committee members as you *conduct the study and write up the results and discussion, with your chair's guidance.* Once your data is collected, you will work closely with your chair regarding the data analysis, results, and discussion. Chairs vary in their involvement (some love to see the data; others prefer you have worked more with the data, results, and interpretation before bringing it to them). They may also refer you to a specific committee member with statistical expertise to help with analysis. It is wise to review the results (perhaps in table or bullet point format) before writing this up formally, as there are often other ways to examine the data, and you want to make sure your interpretation is correct before spending a lot of time writing this. Typically, the chair will review drafts of the results and discussion (along with the revised version of the introduction and methods) a number of times, and then may suggest sending along a more polished copy to the committee members for revision. Once the chair and committee feel your dissertation writing is complete, then you will schedule your oral defense.

It is particularly helpful to *prepare for the oral defense with the help of your chair.* You need to get specific advice about what to prepare, and what the norms and expectations are in the department. For example, typically you do a presentation (which lasts about ten to thirty minutes) which summarizes your study design and findings. You should also be prepared to answer questions about your dissertation and research in general from committee members based on their area of expertise. These questions can be tough, particularly about statistical analyses. In preparation, attend other student's dissertation defenses, or if you can't attend, talk to your peers about their defense experiences. Ask your chair to do a *practice* defense together, so they can review your presentation materials and you can practice answers to commonly asked questions. This will help you identify revisions for the presentation, rehearse speaking clearly and concisely about your topic, and anticipate how to answer questions so you are not (as) surprised. Ultimately, a good dissertation chair wants you to succeed at your defense (even if they do ask difficult questions).

See Table 7b for a list of best practices to use with your dissertation chair and committee members.

Challenges and Changes

Ideally, it would be great to have a strong, conflict-free relationship with your chair and committee. Most of us are not that lucky or that delusional. In fact, part of the committee's job is to question, challenge, and critique your work, to ensure quality. In response, part of your job is to incorporate improvements from multiple parties, but also to be able to articulate and defend your ideas. Different viewpoints and ideas are bound to happen. Lively discussion and disagreements can be fruitful in academics; sometimes, a stronger design or interpretation comes from this pressure. So it is normal to have some degree of conflict, disagreement, or frustration; it is part of the process.

A common fear for students is that they cannot get along with the chair or committee members, or that their committee won't get along with each other. It is actually rare that you can't get along *at all.* But it is fairly common to have conflicts. The key is to *problem-solve collaboratively and constructively with your chair and committee.* Usually there are things that can be done to improve the working relationships, but at times, if people are truly unable to work well together, either they drop you or you drop them. This can happen in a variety of ways, either indirectly by a lack of responding, or directly by making a formal change.

In general, *try to make your relationships work.* Put your energy into working well and problem solving with your dissertation chair and committee, not working against each other. Learn as much as you can from these faculty members. Show them that you are a committed student, delivering drafts that are polished and on time, and incorporating feedback respectfully and thoroughly.

If you are having problems with your chair or committee, *consider your role in the process.*

- Are you following your dissertation work plan regarding timelines and communication? If you haven't worked out some of the details of the plan, or you don't have an agreement in place, it is time to revisit this.
- Are you being diplomatic and assertive in your interactions, rather than passive or aggressive?
- Are you asking for clear feedback and implementing the changes as suggested?
- Are you being realistic about the dissertation process? For example, look at Worksheet 7.2, which lists all of the key steps in a dissertation process. It is not unusual for steps in the dissertation process to have multiple revisions and changes. Most dissertations take several years from concept to completion. See what the norms are for your peers and at your department to get an accurate time estimate. It usually takes more time, work, and revisions to complete a dissertation than students initially think, and it is part of the research process to have challenges.

Make sure you know the norms of the department, what is typical from these faculty members, and the dissertation process in general. You could ask a trusted friend, successful student, or colleague to help you evaluate the situation, get support, and problem-solve ideas about how to respectfully resolve the issues.

However, it is also important to consider your chair and committee member's role in the process and in the dissertation work plan. *There may be times when it is appropriate to consider getting a new dissertation chair or committee member.* For example, if your dissertation chair is recruited to another university or you both mutually agree that it would be better to shift to another dissertation chair, this is a relatively straightforward decision. However, if it is a personality clash, philosophical difference, or lack of direction or availability, this is more challenging. Making a change to your committee is not a decision to be taken lightly, although it sometimes is appropriate, and you will want to weigh the pros and cons carefully. The key is to work to improve relationships when possible, and move forward with new members, if needed. Your approach would be different depending on the type of problem and relationships.

Specific Challenges with Committee Members

If you are having trouble with a particular committee member, work with your chair to figure out the best approach to resolve this problem. For example, it is not uncommon that a committee member may completely disagree with a major design decision. Your chair may feel strongly that you should defend your original design, or after considering the feedback, your chair may suggest a discussion to compromise or change the design. Depending on the relationship, your chair may advocate that you discuss this yourself (via e-mail or meeting) with the faculty member. Or the chair may want to consult with them independently, or call a meeting for all involved to come to resolution. If problems continue, the faculty member is unreasonable, or there is no improvement at problem-solving attempts, then your chair may guide you to investigate other committee members. This is politically tricky; just as you don't want to quit one job before you get another, you want to make sure that there are other faculty members who could appropriately serve on your committee before letting a committee member go. Of course, you don't want to advertise widely that you are *firing* a committee member, or talk negatively about a person in the department. You will need to be discreet and professional when talking with other potential committee members. Work with your chair to determine who to approach and how to officially alert and change committee members.

Specific Challenges with Your Dissertation Chair

If you are having trouble with your dissertation chair, this is a more politically charged issue. A common problem is that a student is not getting clear feedback in a timely manner. First, it is probably best to meet directly and individually with your chair to try to come to some resolution. Second, revisit and revise your dissertation work plan so that you are on the same page about time lines and communication. Third, see if there are things that you could do differently or ways you could work more effectively together. For example, if your chair is very busy during spring semester, but has more time during the summer months, set up more frequent meetings then. Perhaps the chair would be able to respond more quickly to shorter, focused questions in e-mail rather than rereading long drafts or delaying meetings because of a packed schedule. Be realistic for your expectations from busy faculty members and consider what other students typically experience (and live to tell about).

If things are still not improving after multiple attempts, privately consider several things. 1) Are there are other available faculty members who could serve as your chair? 2) Would these other options be considerably better than the current chair (i.e., don't get out of the frying pan and into the fire!) 3) What are the short—and long-term implications of disconnecting with the current chair? For example, it may be frustrating to have delays in feedback, but if you are eventually getting good critical advice from a respected faculty member, it may be worth it. Also, if you break ties with your current dissertation chair, there may be ramifications for your long-term career. Remember that recommendations are important for future jobs and word of mouth, positive or negative, goes a long way in academic circles. However, if you are truly not making any progress on your dissertation, it is unlikely you would get a glowing letter of recommendation anyway.

Before making any official move, talk confidentially with your academic advisor (if different from your chair), your director of training, or the chair of your department to see if they have any advice for you. There may be some additional steps they suggest to try to resolve the situation. Once you have examined all the options, if you decide to move forward with changing your dissertation chair, consider the advice given above. Don't officially ask for an official change in your dissertation chair before solidifying the commitment of another faculty member, and be discreet and professional. Remember that changing your dissertation chair or committee members is not the end of the world. Regroup, try to learn from the experience, and keep moving forward with your dissertation for successful completion.

Conclusion

So the story ends happily for me. I stayed at the university and chose a new dissertation chair who allowed me to investigate a creative area of research. He had a different perspective and a different style than my first chair. However, his good advice for selecting committee members with statistics and methodological expertise, content expertise, and process expertise helped me have a strong proposal and a successful project.

Ultimately, I benefited from having this variety in research experiences. I learned different styles of mentoring, and I broadened my own research areas and interests. I have applied this knowledge about different areas of research and approaches to mentoring now to help other students. And it certainly helped to stay in contact after graduation with both chairs. They both assisted me in different ways to navigate the nuances of the academic world, find rewarding jobs, and ultimately advance in those positions. For that is what good chairs do—whether near or far, they offer sage advice, helpful feedback, and great recommendation letters.

WORKSHEET 7.1: Self-assessment and Faculty Qualities

Qualities	Self-assessment: What do I need/want?	Questions to consider when investigating specific faculty members:	Notes on specific faculty members:
Content area knowledge	List your possible topic areas of interest:	-Is interested in your content area or something similar? -Does research in a specific content area? -Has published in content area? -Teaches about a specific content area? -Has current research projects or grants in your area of interest? -Has national reputation (publications, conferences, grants, and consultancy) for content area knowledge?	
Availability	Write down what time/meetings/avail ability you need from a chair in the short term (weekly/monthly), as well as long term (how long are you going to be in the program):	-Is available on a regular basis for consultation? How frequently? -Is available during certain time frames/semesters? -Has other responsibilities that impact availability (teaching, other students, research, grants, travel, and personal life)? -Enjoys and values mentoring? (Or do they have other responsibilities that they have to give more priority to?) -Is available for length of estimated time to do dissertation (several years)? -Is going on sabbatical? Any plans to leave the university?	
Compatibility	Write down some qualities of leaders/teachers/chairs who you have worked effectively with in the past (formal vs. more casual; provided close oversight vs. allowed more independence):	-Encourages in a positive way? Willing to share their advice, information, wisdom, and experience? -Provides detailed, constructive criticism to improve projects? -Has a style that matches what you value and need (hands-on vs. more freedom; organized or more spontaneous)? -Do you respect this person's opinion and get along with them professionally? -Do they get along well with other faculty members you are considering for your committee?	

Resources	List some resources that would be helpful for you to conduct your study (participants, computer programs, assessments or measures):	-Has current research projects/grants (or plans) that could assist you in completing your dissertation? -Has connections to the sample population that could assist you in completing your dissertation? -Has tangible resources (lab space, computer programs, library of relevant research articles, and access to participants) that could help you complete your dissertation? -Has other (less tangible) connections in the department, university, nationally? (E.g., they are up for department chair next year, they just served as national president for a scientific organization, or have a history of successful grant writing.)	
Specialized skills	Write down the range of skills/ consultants who could help you complete your dissertation (statistical help, expert in methods, connection to participants, editing):	-Has expertise in the method or design that you are considering? -Has statistical expertise to help direct your analyses? -Has access to the participant population you want to use?	
Experience with mentoring other dissertation students	Write down what you are looking for in a chair, as it relates to the process (has mentored lots of students, or only has a few students; makes sure the product is high quality, which may take more time, or allows more flexibility/ variability).	-What is their reputation in the department/university for mentoring students? -What experience have they had as a chair or committee member? -How many students do they currently have? -What do their current and former students say about their mentoring style and experience? -How long do their students typically take to complete their dissertations?	

Table 7b: Best Practices for Working with Your Dissertation Chair and Committee Members

On the topic of . . .	Do	Don't
Roles	Do consult your chair and defer to their judgment in most cases, as they are your primary advisor, liaison, and consultant. Keep them in the loop about all decisions and changes. Set up the expectation up front that the chair will be cc'ed on all communication.	Do not get into challenging situations in which you are meeting independently with other committee members (behind the scenes or behind your chair's back), other faculty members, or other editors for primary guidance on your dissertation. It only sets you up for a political battle if your chair does not agree with their suggestions. If your chair suggests that you consult someone individually, keep your chair informed about the outcome of the meeting. If a committee member sends you something, and the chair not involved or cc'ed, send it to chair to ask for assistance and guidance about how to respond.
Time lines	Do follow your dissertation work plan. Make sure that the dates for short-and long-term goals match your chair and committee's schedule. Without clear communication, you could be surprised when one of your committee members is out of the country for a scientific conference (which had been planned for a year), during a critical period of your dissertation development or defense. Do develop a calendar that lists out small, manageable tasks for yourself, once you have gotten consensus from your chair and committee members about your goals. Break down each part of the dissertation into clear action items. Post this in a place that is visible to you. Do your best to meet the agreed upon deadlines. If you say you will have a draft completed by a certain date, prove that you are a responsible and trustworthy professional by turning in high-quality work on time.	Don't be surprised if the time line needs to change, based on unexpected changes (e.g., one of your recruitment sites is not available, thus delaying data collection; proposal needs some additional revisions and resubmission). Adjust as needed, and keep everyone informed. Don't wait until the last minute to schedule meetings. It is challenging to get busy faculty members together with semester deadlines and research activities. Allow enough time to do this; don't expect people to be available based on your personal needs.

Meetings	Do set regular meetings to keep you accountable and moving forward.	Don't set meetings just for the sake of meeting.
	Do send documents ahead of time for each meeting (a draft of a new chapter; outline of your results), with plenty of time for review before the meeting. Figure out in advance who has to be at meetings (your chair alone or whole committee at key points to get consensus).	Don't be unprepared for meetings. Treat that time with courtesy. By distributing drafts and agenda ahead of time, you give your committee the opportunity to consider the issues beforehand. Working drafts don't have to be perfect; you can have questions/comments throughout, but do make sure the grammar and spelling are correct to help with readability.
	Do make sure you have an agenda with your questions and proposed solutions or pros/cons for decisions. This helps move the meeting along efficiently and shows you have done your homework and have independent thinking.	Don't have meetings without a document to review or agenda to guide you. Bring extra copies. Otherwise, meetings may be vague and unfocused. It is much easier for people to respond to clear questions rather than general ones, and without this, you may get suggestions that are far afield from what you expected.
		Don't leave the meeting without a plan for the next actionable steps and a plan for the next meeting or communication.
	Do plan to meet early and often in the beginning phases of the process so that you and your chair/committee members can reach a consensus. The time to identify and work out problems regarding the method and design is during the development of the proposal. It is much better to do this early rather than to wait until the data is collected and you are trying to defend your dissertation.	
	Do keep detailed notes (or negotiate about who is responsible for keeping notes) during key meetings so all suggestions and plans are noted and recorded. Keep a running list of changes needed, track your progress, and circulate as needed.	
Feedback	Do expect that your chair and committee will give you feedback in a (relatively) timely manner. Try to submit items during times (e.g., class or other prescribed time frames) so that faculty members have time that is reserved for this purpose and revisions are expected.	Don't expect your chair and committee members to rush to meet your deadlines if they are not realistic or just because you suddenly need to graduate. Faculty members are not available all the time. They are busy people too (with classes, research, other students, travel); don't make unrealistic demands.

	If you haven't heard from your committee about a feedback as agreed upon in your dissertation work plan, diplomatically e-mail again or offer to call/meet at a time that is convenient to them to get the feedback. Be courteous and flexible.	
Revisions	Do ask for specific direction and clear feedback on changes.	Don't spend lots of time developing something if you haven't met and cleared your ideas with your chair and, if suggested, the committee. Don't proceed with revising something if you are not clear about the recommended changes. Don't get stuck either; ask for clarification and examples as needed.
	Do expect that you will revise your dissertation proposal and results many, many times as a result of feedback from the chair, committee members, and outside reviewers. Do (try to) be thankful that someone read and thought about your writing long enough to give you feedback.☒	Do not take criticisms as personal attacks. Ultimately, revisions are designed to improve the project. It is better to get comments on your drafts than to identify problems during the defense or realize later that the work is not publishable. Sometimes people are devastated by critiques. Develop thick skin, recognize that everyone in the research business has to undergo reviews (for job talks, grants, publications), and it is designed to strengthen the final product. The process may be painful, but it is for the good of the research (though admittedly sometimes the wording can be a bit harsh—don't take it personally!)
	Do recognize that there will be times that you don't agree with your chair and committee members. This happens on any team, any project, and any grant review.	Don't speak with them or other people disparagingly about your chair or other committee members, You may not agree, and you can engage in thoughtful discussions with them directly. State your viewpoint and rationale assertively. Problem-solve with them about how things can be revised. Recognize that you need to pick your battles, and that sometimes you may have to compromise along the way.
	Do keep a running list of revisions and who suggested them so that you are being responsive to revisions needed. This helps you to keep track and check them off as you go.	

Progress/ Problems	Do keep chair and committee up to date about progress and problems via agreed upon communication methods (e-mail, brief meetings, etc.). Check in frequently, based on agreed upon time frames (weekly, biweekly). Don't let a month go by without some communication.	Don't let too much time go by (e.g., disappear for a year, and then try to explain lack of progress). It is better to let them know if you are struggling professionally or personally, which puts things in context. On the other hand, also don't send a random question or complaint every day. Try to organize your thoughts and send an e-mail or have a meeting when you can resolve multiple questions for a more efficient process.
	Do ask if your chair recommends other services to assist with your dissertation completion, if you are running into difficulties. For example, there may be a university writing center, statistical consultant, dissertation coach, or editor who could legitimately help you along the way.	Don't make excuses or provide too much personal details (your chair is not your personal therapist); focus on what positives you have accomplished, and ask for clear guidance and consultation for dissertation-related problems.

Worksheet 7.2: Dissertation Work Plan: Tasks and Time Line

Phases	Specific Tasks	Involves which members?	Target Date	Actual Date
Pre-IRB	Send draft of Introduction/Literature review to . . .			
	Receive revisions from . . .			
	Incorporate revisions to Introduction/Literature review			
	Send draft of Methods chapter to . . .			
	Receive revisions from . . .			
	Incorporate revisions to Methods			
	Send revised proposal to committee and set up proposal defense			
	Have meeting to defend proposal and plan as a committee			
	Make revisions based on proposal meeting and confirm proposal is ready for outside review/IRB review			
	Submit proposal for IRB review or other outside review process			
	Others:			
Post-IRB	Receive IRB permission			
	Start data collection			
	Complete data collection			
	Analyze data			
	Send draft of Results chapter to . . .			
	Receive revisions from . . .			
	Incorporate revisions to Results			
	Send draft of Discussion chapter to . . .			
	Receive revisions from . . .			
	Incorporate revisions to Discussion			
	Others:			
Oral defense	Circulate final draft . . .			
	Confirm dissertation is ready for oral defense			
	Submit paperwork to schedule oral defense			
	Prepare oral defense presentation			
	Practice oral defense with . . .			
	Complete oral defense with . . .			

	Should be Others:			
Post-oral defense	Make revisions suggested during oral defense			
	Get final approval on dissertation (circulate if needed)			
	Submit dissertation to university and other paperwork to graduate!			
	Adapt dissertation work into publishable manuscript			
	Others:			

Work with your chair and committee members to tailor the timing, order, focus, and committee members involved in these tasks, depending on the regulations of your department and the suggestions of the committee. Note that the revisions and feedback process may occur multiple times for certain tasks, as needed. Make sure to build in plenty of time for each step, and anticipate that the target dates may have to be adjusted along the way.

Worksheet 7.3: Dissertation Work Plan: Contact Information

Name	Role	Phone Numbers*	E-mail Addresses*	Mailing Address
	Student	Cell:		
		Office:		
		Home:		
	Chair	Cell:		
		Office:		
		Home:		
	Committee Member	Cell:		
		Office:		
		Home:		
	Committee Member	Cell:		
		Office:		
		Home:		
	Committee Member	Cell:		
		Office:		
		Home		

Indicate which phone number and e-mail address is preferred for each member. Please note that some individuals may not want to be contacted at home.

"The ability to use the library to research sources properly and knowledgeable about APA formatting. I think being a critical thinker would come in second. . . . For me, to research a topic or to narrow a topic to something of interest, the first step is always the lit review."

"Every day do at least one thing that moves your dissertation forward. Have a list of a zillion little steps that will move you forward (download articles to read at the dentist, delete words you don't need in your proposal, etc.). Often, if you take one step, that will help to build momentum for other steps. It is easy to get off track and get off the train. That is when you get into trouble. Life happens, family problems happen; don't stay stuck. Do one little thing today to get back on track."

"How to write in a scholarly style. Struggling with learning research AND learning to write is a prescription for pain and suffering, if not failure."

"As a dissertation chair, what's the one thing you wish every mentee knew?"

"The importance of getting the problem statement, purpose statement and research questions to be exactly what you want to study. Use these are your guide to help keep you on track as you are writing."

"The importance of alignment between the key elements of the proposal (title, problem, purpose, research questions, interview questions, hypotheses, survey) must be in perfect alignment. The study is often dynamic and changes during the process. Therefore, the researcher should periodically review to ensure that the elements are still aligned and make revisions as needed."

"This is your project, and your chair and committee are there to help guide you. Take ownership of your dissertation just as you would a big project at work that you are in charge of."

"That the dissertation is on a separate course track than the course track, they need to be working on both. Often, students think they can complete the course track and the dissertation takes care of itself."

CHAPTER 8

Hints for Success from a Quality and IRB Perspective

Linda de Charon, PhD

At times, the process of writing your dissertation feels like a solitary journey. Safely tucked into your office, you work alone, and you write what you consider to be your best work. You are passionate about the topic; you become immersed. But there comes a time when your dissertation is supposed to be shared. At some point, you have to send your work out into the world to be reviewed. And that can be scary, especially if you are not sure whether you have written and formatted your dissertation in a way that it will be well received. What if it is critiqued? (Be prepared, it will be.) What if the reviewers suggest a thousand changes? (It may feel like this).

Many students are initially overwhelmed by the reviews they get from chairs, committee members, or outside reviewers. However, keep in mind that getting a critical review of your work is an important part of the academic process to strengthen the proposal and ultimately to improve the scholarly contribution you are making. You get several chances to practice this skill along the way during your dissertation journey. Learning how to anticipate critiques as well as how to appropriately respond to them will help you to become a better scholar during your doctoral program as well as in your life after graduation when you develop new projects, research, publications, or grants.

One way to successfully navigate the review process is to learn ahead of time what reviewers typically look for, so that you can avoid common pitfalls and submit a high-quality product. You don't want to be *shooting in the dark* at a target that is not clear. That is where I hope to be helpful—by providing clear targets for you. After reviewing hundreds of dissertation proposals and completed dissertations over a number of years, I have seen many themes emerge as common errors and areas of challenge for students developing their dissertations. In this chapter, I outline these issues and describe how to successfully meet many challenges that will be faced along the journey. By reading this chapter, you will get an insider's view of what reviewers look for when reviewing dissertations. By following these guidelines as well as reviewing your own department-specific guidelines and good dissertation examples, you will save time, limit your mistakes, and produce a better scholarly work. Chapter by chapter and section by section, here are suggestions for addressing the issues that you will be encountering.

Avoiding the Common Pitfalls: Chapter by Chapter

The following sections describe issues that are frequently seen during proposal and dissertation reviews. Common problems are discussed for each chapter and each section within that chapter.

- **The Dissertation Proposal**

The dissertation proposal consists of chapters 1 through 3. Students are typically still becoming familiar with the writing requirements during the proposal phase. Therefore, issues include difficulties with learning to write about a study that they intend to accomplish, but without using first-person language. Remember that the proposal should focus on *the study* rather than on what *you* are going to do.

- ■ *The Title*
  - The title of the study is extremely important as it sets the groundwork and the expectations for the reader. A common error made by novice researchers is to include a *catchy* title that expresses their preconceived results. Ensure that the title reflect your *research*, not your expected outcomes. Consider including the design in your title. However, the title should not exceed fifteen words.

- *Chapter 1: The Introduction*

Chapter 1 introduces the proposed study. *Chapter 1* includes the basis for why the study is important, what problem it will address, and how it will contribute to the body of knowledge. The initial chapter also provides a brief overview of the proposed method and design.

- ■ *Introduction Section*
  - Ensure that the introduction section does not include a title other than the chapter title. Exclude any superfluous information in the introduction section—the introduction should be about a one-half to three-fourths page overview of the topic and an overview of chapter 1.

- *Background*
  - The background section should focus on the background *of the problem*. Ensure that the background section is not just a condensed version of the literature review. The discussion should describe the importance of the issue under study and should convince the reader that the proposed research is of value.
- *The Problem Statement*
  - The problem statement should be very clear and concise, and include published support for conducting the proposed study. The section should include both a general problem and a specific problem. Although it is not mandatory, including sentences that begin with "The general problem is . . ." and "The specific problem is . . ." will assist the reviewer in locating these important elements. Otherwise, the general and specific problems can be missed and lead to an unapproved proposal. The specific problem must include a citation. Also, keep in mind that *lack of current studies* or *limited existing research* is not considered a problem in and of itself. The problem statement must be written to reflect an actual problem or issue. Consider what actual issue is occurring due to the lack of current knowledge, or what problem can be resolved as a result of the data to be collected and analyzed within the proposed dissertation. I have seen many proposals submitted with a problem statement that is actually the purpose of the study. It is important to not confuse the problem with the purpose, but also keep in mind that the two should mirror each other. For example, for a *problem* of poor organizational communication the *purpose* might be to examine factors that contribute to the lack of effective communication.
- *The Purpose Section*
  - Frequently, novice researchers will use the purpose section to discuss *what* will occur during the study and *how* the study will be conducted. However, the *purpose* section needs to focus on *why*. Why is the study being proposed? What are the objectives of the study? This section must discuss the research method, design, variables if applicable, geographic location, and the population under study.
- *Significance of the Study*
  - As implied by the section title, the significance of the study section should describe why the proposed study is significant, and to whom. Consider how the research will contribute to the existing body of knowledge and who the information may benefit.
- *The Nature of the Study*
  - The "nature of the study" section should describe at length how the proposed research design will accomplish the goals and why other possible research designs will not fully meet these objectives. Consider

what your proposed method and design will accomplish that cannot be accomplished with an alternative method or design.

- *Research Questions*
  - All studies must include research questions, which are overarching questions that represent the research goals. Do not confuse research questions with the interview questions that are asked directly to the participants. The research questions must be open-ended questions, such as beginning with *what* or *how*. Ensure that the research questions align well with the purpose of the study. One research question is sufficient for a quantitative study, but qualitative research should include two or three research questions. If the intent of the study is to develop a model or theory, include a research question such as "What model (or theory) might (explain, improve) . . . ?"

- *Hypotheses*
  - Hypotheses are used in quantitative studies to predict the outcomes of a study. Each set of hypotheses should include a null and alternate (also known as *alternative*) statement. If the literature supports an expected direction of difference, then the alternate hypotheses should state the expected outcome. If the direction of difference is unexpected, then the alternate hypotheses should seek a *significant* difference. The sets of hypotheses should be listed beginning with the null statement (H0) and then the alternate (HA). Issues that I have seen as a reviewer include students who plan to test hypotheses using only descriptive statistics. If you are planning to include hypotheses and do not understand the concept of inferential statistics, either plan to work with a statistician or a committee member who does understand how to appropriately test hypotheses or consider using a qualitative method instead.

- *Theoretical Framework*
  - The theoretical framework should provide a set of theories that underlie the study. The framework begins with a broad theoretical foundation that serves as a basis for this study. The theoretical framework discussion should begin very broadly with the foundational theory and narrow toward theories related to specific research purpose—think of moving from the top of a *V* toward the tip. The section should include any controversies among theorists.

- *Scope, Limitations, Delimitations, and Generalizability*
  - The scope should describe the breadth of the study—what will be included and what will be excluded. Limitations are conditions that cannot be controlled by the researcher and delimitations are conditions that are controlled by the researcher. The delimitations impact the generalizability of the findings. Remember to discuss how

the delimitations of your study will impact whether your findings can or cannot be generalized to a broader or different population.

- ***Chapter 2: The Literature Review***

A common pitfall within the literature review is a lack of breadth. The topics discussed in the literature review often focus only on the specific problem. In contrast, the literature should begin by setting the stage for discussion of the literature relevant to the purpose. The reviewed literature should also be synthesized rather than presented as a sequential overview of various sources. The following sections describe frequent issues seen in each section of the literature review and how to prevent them.

- *Introduction Section*
  - The introduction section should not include a separate heading. Briefly reiterate the topic and scope of the study, and then introduce the literature review. Also include an overview of the chapter section.
- *Documentation Overview*
  - Following the chapter 2 introduction, include a section heading such as *Title Searches, Articles, Research Documents, and Journals Researched* or simply *Documentation.* One common option for this section is to include key words searched. Another option is to include a table of search findings, such as the number of journals, books, and dissertations reviewed for each topic addressed in the literature review. Either method should work well, but remember that if the table exceeds a page, it must be moved to an appendix.
- *Formatting the Literature Review*
  - The topics within the literature should flow from broad, general to topics and narrow toward the specific topics related to the purpose of the study. Much like the theoretical framework, the information should be formatted as a *V* progressing from a broad discussion to specific topics. The main section of the literature review should include a historical overview of the various topics, a current overview of those same topics, and any contemporary topics. Previous studies related to the purpose of the study should also be discussed to provide support for the significance of the study being proposed. The following discussion provides detailed information on developing these sections.
- *Historical Overview*
  - Begin with a historical overview section that includes separate subheadings for each topic from the theoretical framework. Begin with the broadest theoretical area that provides the foundation for the theoretical framework. Also review your mind map for any additional

topics that should be included (see chapter 4 for information regarding mind mapping). For quantitative studies, ensure that each study variable is discussed. A good method for delineating between historic information and current information is to include all references over five years old within the historic section. Also ensure that any controversies between theorists are described, but do not indicate support for either position. The literature review must be unbiased.

- *Current Overview*
  - Follow the historical overview section with the same sequence of subheadings as you used in the historical overview section. The current overview should provide a synopsis of contemporary literature on each of the topics or variables. Review your mind map for any additional topics that have been introduced in the literature within the last five years. The current overview should include recent dissertations and cutting-edge information within the field. Again, include any controversies between current theorists while avoiding the perception of bias.

- *Previous Studies*
  - The literature review must include a focus on what has already been accomplished within the field of study. The description must include methods and designs used to previously study the problem and reveal controversies between the researchers, also defined as tensions in the literature. The literature review must present a critical analysis of the existing research, describing the scope and the limitations of studies that have already been accomplished.

- *Literature Gap/Significance of the Proposed Study*
  - The discussion of previous studies and what has already been accomplished within the field of study should provide a basis for the gap in the literature. Describe what still needs to be uncovered, and how your proposed study will assist in closing the current gap in the literature. Discuss how your proposed method and design may be a significant contribution to knowledge within the field of study.

- *Conclusions*
  - The conclusions section should consist of conclusions that you have derived based on your analysis of the literature. The discussion should include the interconnections between the knowledge that currently exists in the field. The section should also place your proposed study within the context of the existing literature.

- *Chapter 2: Summary*
  - The summary section should briefly summarize the key points of the chapter. It is, of course, important to include citations throughout

the summary. Finally, include a transition to chapter 3. Remember to include transition statements at the end of all chapter summaries.

- ***Chapter 3: The Research Method***

The intent of chapter 3 is to provide a detailed discussion of the planned data collection and analysis. This chapter should continue the discussion introduced in the chapter 1 purpose and nature of the study sections. Common pitfalls associated with chapter 3 include a lack of understanding between the terms *method* and *design*, insufficient support for the selected design, a lack of understanding between the terms *population* and *method*, and an insufficient level of detail of the intended the collection and analysis procedures.

- *Introduction*
  - The introduction section should reiterate the purpose of the study. An overview of the chapter should be provided in this section. Also remember to spell out acronyms again to remind the reader of the meaning associated with any unique acronyms.
- *Method and Design*
  - Proper method and design differentiation is very important. Methods include quantitative, qualitative, or mixed method. Ensure that you rationalize why you selected your method, such as qualitative over quantitative or quantitative over qualitative. Keep in mind that the design is more specific than the method. For example, the qualitative method includes case study, narrative inquiry, ethnography, phenomenological, grounded theory, and many other possible designs. Ensure that you are clearly and consistently delineating between the two terms.
- *Design Appropriateness*
  - Once you have properly differentiated between your selected method and design and rationalized selection of your method, you must next support why your selected design is the most appropriate. For example, if you are proposing a case study, you must support the selection of this design based on descriptions from design experts such as Robert Yin. It is important to identify the specific experts associated with your selected design and cite those experts within your rationale. You must also compare the objectives of your design against other similar designs, such as contrast a case study design against other qualitative designs such as narrative inquiry, ethnography, phenomenological, and grounded theory.

- *Research Questions and Hypotheses*
  - In chapter 3, you will need to restate the research questions and hypotheses from chapter 1. Although this sounds simple enough, a common error is that the research questions and hypotheses often do not match between the chapters. Remember to reflect any changes that you make to the research questions or hypotheses in all chapters.
- *Population and Sample*
  - Distinguishing correctly between population and sample is a very common pitfall. Within the population section, describe the criteria for participation and, if possible, provide an estimated number of participants eligible to participate. Within the sample section, describe the actual number of participants and how those participants will be recruited. Remember that population includes those eligible to participate and sample includes only the actual participants. Ensure that you support the proposed sample size for both quantitative and qualitative studies.
- *Informed Consent and Confidentiality*
  - Discussion of the informed consent must be explicit. Whether the participant will sign the informed consent form prior to participation or click on a consent button on a web page to access a survey, chapter 3 must be very specific on how and when consent will be obtained. You need to state that no data will be collected until consent has been obtained. Steps to ensure confidentiality must also be explained, including how the participants will be coded, how long and where the data will be retained, and how and when the data will be destroyed in the future. Although three years is typical, review your university's Institutional Review Board (IRB) form for specific information regarding the required length of secure data retention.
- *Instrument Selection or Development*
  - Clearly state why you selected the instrument—such as survey or questionnaire—that you plan to use to collect your data. If you will be using an existing instrument, compare it to similar instruments and describe your rationale for selection. If you created your own instrument, rationalize how the survey or interview questions will achieve the objectives of the study. Discuss whether any commercially available instruments could have been used and describe the basis for development of the instrument. Also discuss whether your original instrument will undergo any pilot studies or expert panel reviews such as evaluations to confirm the clarity or validity of the questions. Keep in mind that an evaluation is essential for original instruments. Remember to include demographic questions in the instrument such

as gender, occupation, ethnicity, age groups, or other relevant data for chapter 4 demographic reporting of your participants. Include your instrument as an appendix, unless including the instrument will violate copyright laws.

- *Data Collection*
  - The data collection section must be sufficiently detailed to convey how and when the data will be collected. A common issue in this section is a lack of clarity and detail. This section should align well with both the informed consent section and the instrumentation section, and may well include some redundancy with those two sections.
- *Validity, Reliability, Credibility, Transferability, and Dependability*
  - A common error in this section is use of the proper terminology based on the selected method. Validity and reliability should be discussed in support of quantitative studies. Commercially available or existing surveys often have existing validity and reliability data that should be included in chapter 3. If you are creating an original survey, discuss how you will determine validity and reliability (Cronbach's alpha) using a pilot study. However, for a qualitative study, rather than validity and reliability, describe how you will determine trustworthiness such as credibility, transferability, and dependability. References that describe these qualitative trustworthiness concepts include Denzin and Lincoln (2005).
- *Data Analysis*
  - Pitfalls for the data analysis section of chapter 3 include insufficient detail, especially for quantitative methods. For quantitative studies, the section should describe how the null hypotheses will be tested and what criteria will be used to determine whether the null is accepted or rejected. Discuss the statistical tests that will be used, and include *a priori* the level of significance (alpha) that will be used in testing. Keep in mind that the statistical tests may need to be revised based on the actual (as opposed to. planned) sample size.
  - A frequently seen issue for qualitative data analysis is that the specific analysis method proposed in chapter 3 fails to match the actual method used in chapter 4. Two reasons appear to cause this discontinuity. First, students often propose the use of analysis software, then find that the software is to complex or difficult to learn and use. Then in chapter 4, the students will claim to have used the software when clearly they have not. In my experience, about 90% of students propose to use qualitative analysis software, but less than half of those students actually use the software. This can be avoided by reviewing the analysis software closely prior to developing chapter 3. If the sample size will be small, or the software seems too difficult to master or too expensive

to purchase, then propose a manual content analysis. Using a manual process is perfectly acceptable. Several researchers, including Zhang and Wildemuth (2009), have documented specific steps for manual analysis.

- The second issue that often results in a lack of continuity between the proposed qualitative analysis and the analysis actually accomplished is that students frequently reiterate the complex steps listed by a design expert without understanding how these steps are actually implemented. A prime example of this situation is Moustakas' modified van Kaam method of analysis associated with phenomenology. Accomplished as listed, these seven steps require considerable effort; therefore, these frequently proposed seven steps are rarely actually accomplished in dissertations. In this example, consider instead the four steps of Moustakas' modified Stevick-Colaizzi-Keen method. For all data qualitative data analysis, it is imperative to understand the effort involved in the analysis that you are proposing, and propose only what you will actually accomplish.

- *Summary*
  - The summary section of chapter 3 should reiterate the method, design, sample, and planned data collection and analysis. The proposal submission consists of only chapters 1 through 3; therefore, it seems logical to omit a transition to chapter 4. However, include a transition to chapter 4 in the chapter 3 summary.

Taking a Broader Perspective of the Proposal

It is essential to ensure alignment between the key elements of the proposal. In a qualitative study the title, general problem, specific problem, purpose, research questions, and interview questions must be perfectly aligned and support one another. Similarly, in a quantitative study, the title, general problem, specific problem, purpose, research questions, hypotheses, and survey must be in perfect alignment. The study is often dynamic and changes during the process. Therefore, you should periodically review to ensure that the elements are still aligned and make revisions as needed.

The following activity is designed to assist in assuring alignment between your key elements. Remember to revisit this activity if any of those key elements change during the course of your proposal development.

Activity 8.1: **Aligning Your Key Proposal Elements**

- If you are accomplishing a *qualitative* study, use bullets to write the following elements: title, general problem, specific problem, purpose, research questions, and interview questions.
- If you are accomplishing a *quantitative* study, use bullets to write the following elements: title, general problem, specific problem, purpose, research questions, null and alternate hypotheses, and all survey questions.
- Review each element for continuity and alignment. Ensure
  - The title accurately reflects the purpose of the study.
  - The specific problem is a subset of the general problem.
  - The specific problem and purpose mirror each other.
  - The research questions will fully meet the objectives of the purpose.
  - *For qualitative studies*, the interview questions are clearly aligned with the research questions.
  - *For quantitative studies*, the hypotheses are clearly aligned with the research questions, and the survey questions will appropriately address the hypotheses.
- In an electronic document, perform a *find* function on the term *purpose*. Review each stated purpose throughout the document and ensure that the intent is consistent.
- *If you are doing a qualitative study, complete template 8.1a.*
- *If you are doing a quantitative study, complete template 8.1b.*

Activity 8.1a: Aligning your *Qualitative* Study Key Proposal Elements

Study title

_____

General problem

_____

Specific problem

_____

Purpose

_____

Research questions (include two or three)

R1:_____

R2:_____

R3:_____

Interview questions (typically 12)

1._____
2._____
3._____
4._____
5._____
6._____
7._____
8._____
9._____
10._____
11._____
12._____

Activity 8.1b: Aligning your *Quantitative* Study Key Proposal Elements

Study title

_____

General problem

_____

Specific problem

_____

Purpose

_____

Research questions (at least one)

R1:_____

R2:_____

Hypotheses (at least two sets)

$H1_0$:_____
$H1_A$:_____
$H2_0$:_____
$H2_A$:_____
$H3_0$:_____
$H3_A$:_____

Survey questions

1._____
2._____
3._____
4._____
5._____
6._____
7._____
8._____
9._____
10._____
11._____
12._____

Barriers to Overall Clarity

Now that you have successfully avoided the many potential pitfalls associated with developing a proposal and ensured alignment of the key elements throughout your document, you are ready to submit your proposal for approval. Well, almost ready. First, you will need to ensure that your proposal is approved by your dissertation chair and committee. It is important to be aware of the following common barriers to the clarity of the proposal.

- Quantitative data collection and analysis alignment
  - Selecting the definitive statistical tests can be difficult. If the quantitative data to be collected are not analyzed correctly, the results will lack meaning. If there are doubts regarding the correct analysis procedures to use, it will be important to work with a statistician.
- Proximity to the study
  - Being too close to the study can be a huge barrier to ensuring clarity. Often both the student and chair have discussed the study at length and are thoroughly knowledgeable of the intent of the study. However, that closeness can obscure the reality of the written word. Simply understanding the intent is not sufficient; it is imperative that a reader with no verbal background regarding the intent can clearly understand the proposed study.
- Editing issues
  - Even the best proposed study can be negatively impacted by poor grammar, sentence structure issues, and APA (American Psychological Association) formatting errors. Most dissertations will need to be edited at some point. However, depending on the review process used at your university, APA and grammar editing may be part of the university process. Check with your chair to find out if, and when, you should work with an editor.
- Ignoring the *next-door neighbor rule.*
  - Many doctoral students erroneously feel that doctoral level writing requires use of esoteric verbiage—a writing style that is overly complex and understandable only by the most educated. While the writing must be scholarly and colloquial language must be avoided, consider the importance of the *next-door neighbor rule.* The writing should be so straightforward that your friends, adult family members, or next-door neighbor can read and understand your dissertation.

Activity 8.2: Identifying Individuals to Review Your Dissertation

- Consider the four barriers to clarity:
  - Quantitative data collection and analysis alignment
  - Proximity to the study
  - Editing issues
  - Ignoring the *next-door neighbor rule*
- List appropriate individuals that can assist you in overcoming the barriers applicable to your study by reviewing your proposal and dissertation. Consider committee members, friends and family, assistance available at local universities, and professional resources.

Activity 8.2: Identifying Individuals to Review your Dissertation

Questions for Reflection	Potential Resources
☐ What are the strengths of each of my committee members?	
☐ Who understands my topic well?	
☐ Who has the ability to recognize potential alignment issues in the proposal design?	
☐ Who will review for APA and grammar?	
☐ Do I need to hire an editor?	
☐ Do I need a statistician?	
☐ Which friends or family members would be willing to read and provide honest feedback?	

Completing the Study: The Final Dissertation Chapters

Congratulations for arriving at this point! By now you have an approved proposal, have collected and analyzed your data, and are ready to write the final chapters. Depending on the study design, you may well have more than five chapters. However, most dissertations will include only the five chapters. This section will provide hints for successful completion of the dissertation document, including chapters 4 and 5.

- **Revising the Proposal Chapters**

Chapters 1 through 3 were written in future tense with regard to the proposed study. Now that the study is complete, revise the grammar to past tense. In the electronic document, perform a *find* on *proposed, proposal, will,* and any other terms need to be revised to reflect a completed study.

Also revise anything that did not actually occur according to the proposed plan. This includes the sample size and any planned statistical tests that were changed from the proposed study. Review chapters 1 and 3 for any items that need to be revised to reflect the research as it actually occurred.

- **Chapter 4: Analysis and Results**

Chapter 4 must focus only on the analysis and results. Common errors include reiteration of the method and design information from chapter 3 and including citations for the data collection and analysis procedures. All support for the data collection and analysis should be stated in chapter 3 rather than chapter 4. Also ensure that the data are presented without bias and without applying meaning to the data. Any conclusions must be saved for chapter 5. The following sections describe important items to remember while developing chapter 4.

- Introduction
  - Begin chapter 4 with a reintroduction to the purpose of the study. Again, remember to spell out any unique acronyms. Then provide an overview of the chapter.
- Pilot Study
  - Following the introduction, describe any pilot study or reviews that were accomplished in advance of developing the final instrument. Include the number of participants or reviewers and describe the specific changes that were made to the survey or questionnaire as a result.

- Demographics
    - This is why it was important to include demographics questions in the instrument! Chapter 4 should include a section that describes the demographics of the participants. However, it is imperative that the demographics are shown in a way that maintains participant confidentiality. Rather than narrative or an integrated table that indicate data specific to each participant—such as participant 001 is female, Caucasian, holds a master's degree, and has twelve years of experience—include small tables that address the demographics questions separately, without linking the information to a specific participant. For example, provide separate tables for gender, race, education levels, and experience levels.
- Data Collection
    - The data collection section should describe how the data were collected. Essentially, the information will be much like the data collection section in chapter 3, but this version should reflect reality—how it really happened. You may be surprised how different reality will be from the original plan, and here you can share that story with the reader.
- Data Analysis
    - The data analysis section is central to chapter 4. It is important to recognize that the data analysis procedures discussion must be detailed enough that another researcher could replicate the results. For quantitative studies, describe how the null hypotheses statements were tested. For qualitative studies, describe the basis of how the themes emerged. Again, ensure that the data analysis method described in chapter 4 matches chapter 3. If the originally proposed analysis was not the analysis that actually occurred, then revise it in chapter 3 (with your chair's approval, of course).
- Results
    - For quantitative studies, state the results of the analysis, including tables and figures as appropriate. For qualitative studies, include short key phrases from the participants to support the themes. If you use qualitative analysis software, include the software output, such as frequencies and nodes. As stated earlier, it is common to have students propose the use of a qualitative analysis software but develop themes without any support for how the themes were developed. Those students are required to revise and resubmit their dissertation to demonstrate how they used the software, or to remove the discussion of the software and state how the themes were developed manually. It is an important pitfall to avoid!

- *Tables*: Common errors associated with tables are formatting issues. Per APA, tables should only include horizontal lines. It is also important to format the table title using upper and lower case, italicized font. Also, do not split the tables across pages; either create smaller tables to fit on a single page or move the entire table to an appendix.
- *Figures*: As with tables, the common errors associated with figures are also APA formatting issues. Use grayscale only, no color, and do not use 3-D views since they only complicate the conveyance of the information. Any text within the figure itself must be a sans serif font, such as Arial or Calibri, and the text must be a minimum of 8-point and a maximum of 14-point font. Additionally, the figure captions should be sentence case ending with a period and should be fully descriptive and explanatory. Do not split the figure and caption across pages.

- Chapter 4: Summary
  - The summary of chapter 4 must reiterate the results of the study. Restate the results of the hypotheses testing or the emergent themes. Be cautious not to attribute meaning to the results at this point. Then conclude with a transition to chapter 5. You are very close to completing at this point . . . keep up that momentum!

- **Chapter 5: Conclusions and Recommendations**

Finally, the last chapter of the long doctoral journey! Again, some designs may include more than five chapters, but most will conclude with chapter 5. All of the writing up to this point has been based on the synthesis of other theorist's views and other researcher's studies. This is the time to finally allow your own voice to be heard—your conclusions and recommendations based on the results of your study.

- Introduction
  - Begin chapter 5 with a reiteration of the purpose of the study, spell out any unique acronyms, and briefly remind the reader of the results from chapter 4. Then provide an overview of the final chapter.
- Research Question Findings
  - Students frequently become so focused on the hypotheses results and emergent themes that they forget to address the research questions. Those are the research questions that drove the research in chapters 1 and 3. Discuss the research question findings and align the hypotheses results and emergent themes with those questions.
- Implications of the Findings
  - It is important to align the study results with the chapter 2 literature. Include a subsection heading for each hypotheses or theme from chapter 4. For each hypotheses finding or each emergent theme, compare and contrast your results to the findings of past researchers discussed in the chapter 2 literature review.
- Limitations
  - In contrast to chapter 1, which described the *expected* conditions that could not be controlled, the limitations section of chapter 5 should discuss additional limitations of the study discovered during the research. What limitations actually hindered accomplishing the study? For example, was the planned sample size obtained? Did you have access to all of the participants that you were hoping to interview? Were you able to collect as much data as originally planned? And how did those limitations impact the study?
- Recommendations for Action
  - Based on your study findings, describe what leaders in your field might do to address the problem that originally drove the study. Provide specific, actionable recommendations that might assist leaders to mitigate the problem in the future. Consider including a model, a diagram that depicts the recommendations relative to the problem or depicts your recommended solutions leading to an improved end state. A clear model is a magnificent contribution to literature and can easily become the basis for a journal article or even a book!
- Recommendations for Further Research
  - The recommendations for future research section should include a few specific recommendations for other researchers. Include a recommended method, design, and focus for further studies that might advance knowledge within the field based on gaps in literature that you have uncovered. Also consider how you would have improved your study given unlimited resources or access.

- Chapter 5: Summary
  - In the summary, reiterate the goals of the study and research question findings. State the significance of those findings and how your study has contributed to the body of knowledge in your field. Also describe the potential benefits that could be derived from your recommendation for action or by implementing your original model.

Abstract

As you complete the chapter 5 summary, also begin developing the abstract page. Per APA, do not indent the abstract. Develop a single paragraph up to 250 words that clearly states the purpose, method, design, sample size, and findings of the study. Also consider including recommendations, potential benefits of the study, or how the research has contributed to the body of knowledge. Although the abstract takes up very little space, it serves an important function, forcing you to summarize the key points of your study. The abstract is often the first (and sometimes the only) thing that is read about your study, so make certain that it communicates an interesting and accurate depiction of your work.

Summary

These hints for success were developed based on several years of reviewing proposals and dissertation in the hope of assisting you in avoiding the most common errors. Remember that the fewer errors that you make during the development of your proposal and final dissertation, the sooner you will receive proposal and dissertation approval. Although the journey is part of your growth process as a doctoral scholar, completing that journey as soon as possible is an astonishing feeling, not to mention the tuition that you will save!

CHAPTER 9

Oral Defense

Ron Hutkin, PhD; and Timothy Delicath, PhD

Introduction

The purpose of this chapter is to discuss the oral defense of the completed dissertation, the types of formats for the oral defense, and some of the frequently asked questions about the oral defense. While many doctoral students fret and lose sleep prior to the big day, the demeanor should be just the opposite. Look at it this way.

By the time you complete your study, who is the expert on your topic, you or the committee? Who knows more about the intricate details of your study than you? And who, other than you, is in a better position to discuss the conclusions and recommendations of the study?

Save the Best for Last

You all know the saying "It is the best of times, and it is the worst of times." While stressing over collecting data, not getting a good response rate on surveys, or having interviews cancelled may have challenges and could be called the worst of times, getting ready for the oral defense should be likened to the best of times.

So what do you do during the oral defense about articulating a low return rate on surveys or interviews that may go astray? You talk honestly, openly, and candidly about what happened and the probable reasons to explain what happened. If you try to cover up or ignore this kind of condition, it will be the worst of times. On the other hand, your data might reveal some outliers or unexpected results that not only add importance to the study but also generate some wonderful ideas and recommendations for further research. Discussing your study in general and such things as outliers in specific will be the best of times. Let's talk about common formats for the oral defense and how to prepare for the best of times.

Preparing for the Event

The good news is that you have been preparing for your dissertation defense since you started the program. Your hard work developing and writing your dissertation will lead you to a successful defense. Most chairs and committee members will not let you schedule your defense until they are reasonably confident that you will do a good job, and the work is polished. So you have years of preparation on your side.

There are some additional things you will need to do to prepare for a successful defense day. First, make sure you have talked with your chair about exactly what to prepare (presentation, what questions to anticipate, what format to use, what materials to circulate, the logistics). Second, find out who to invite; some universities and departments require outside or appointed reviewers; some allow colleagues and friends to attend. You will coordinate with committee members about setting the date, once you get the blessing from your chair. Don't be surprised if it takes a while to get a date for all of the relevant players; faculty members tend to be very busy.

Prepare your presentation materials and practice (practice, practice!), with trusted friends or colleagues. Consider what questions you may have to answer during the Q & A. Have friends and colleagues try to *stump* you with tough questions so that you can practice handling these with grace. Use Worksheet #1 to help with your presentation practice and Worksheet #2 to anticipate common questions in the Q & A session (discussed later in this chapter).

As the day of defense approaches, make sure you have extra copies of everything (on electronic devices/drives and hard copy materials) and notes for easy reference during the defense. Have a paper and pen to jot down questions and list recommended changes during the process. Get to the room/location early to set up so that you feel comfortable there. Practice relaxation techniques, if you are feeling anxious (deep breathing, take a walk, prayer or meditation, etc.). Make sure you have eaten well and have water available in case you get thirsty (plus taking a drink is a great way to pause to consider a difficult question). But perhaps the best preparation is a good night's sleep in order to be alert, sharp, and to demonstrate and articulate your competence and expertise.

The Format: Conference Tabling or PowerPointing

There are two common formats for the oral defense: First, a live setting in a conference or meeting room with a PowerPoint presentation. Second, a conference call, along with a computer-assisted PowerPoint presentation. Let's visit about each one. Conducting the oral defense in a conference room is typical for on campus brick-and-mortar programs. You and your chair will agree on a time and place for the oral defense. In this situation, the committee will have either a hard copy or an electronic copy of your completed dissertation. In a few instances, the oral defense may be conducted in a classroom or lecture hall with open invitations extended to other faculty and students. Your attire for the oral defense would be business attire, suit and tie for men and suit with skirt or slacks for women along with nicely shined shoes for all.

For online programs, the oral defense is usually conducted with a conference call along with a PowerPoint presentation and the completed dissertation distributed by electronic means. These documents should be sent to the committee at least seven days in advance of the defense. Again, the day and time is usually determined by the student and the committee as well as being agreeable to the other members of the committee. Twenty PP slides, excluding references, are usually considered the optimal. Here is the reason. A general rule of thumb is that it takes about ninety seconds to discuss and explain the content of the slide. So, with twenty slides, your discussion of the dissertation would take about thirty minutes. Experience has shown that is just about right. Your attire for the oral defense can be whatever is comfortable, unless you also have the computer cameras turned on.

Although there are some differences in these two oral defense formats, there are some commonalities. After a few introductions, and perhaps some small talk, the chair will bring the committee to order and then turn the meeting over to you for the presentation and defense of your doctoral dissertation research study. Here is what committees want to know whether you are in person or online.

- The statement of the problem and why it is significant or important
- How the literature supports the need for the study
- The research design
- The hypotheses and/or research questions
- The analysis of the data and statistics used
- The findings
- The conclusions
- The unexpected results or outliers
- The recommendations for further research

All of this information from the student will be followed by the Q & A part of the oral defense. Some chairs will conduct the Q & A on an individual basis, and others on a round-robin basis.

Common (and Not so Common) Questions during the Q & A Session

Although the presentation has its own challenges (Do the slides look okay? Am I going too fast?), many students feel more anxiety about the Q & A section of the defense. Perhaps this is because you feel you have less control over this part of the process. It is indeed hard to predict all of the questions that will be raised during the Q & A session. However, you can control how much you prepare and anticipate the questions beforehand. You can talk with your chair and committee members ahead of time to see if there are any tips or suggestions they have for this part of the defense (common questions, etc.). You can predict, in general, which faculty members may be more or less helpful, and what their typical interests/questions are. You can practice answering difficult questions with friends and colleagues. You can control the way you respond in session, carefully and honestly. So there are concrete things you can do to help yourself be as prepared as possible for the Q & A session, giving you some semblance of control and predictability.

Common Questions

This section is designed to help you think through and prepare for some of the common questions that arise during a defense. By going through these questions in your mind beforehand, writing out some answers and notes, and practicing your responses with a trusted colleague or friend, you will feel better about the process. Here are some frequently used questions:

- What is your next step with this research? Discuss future research studies.
- What is the biggest limitation or weakness in your dissertation?
- What would you do differently if you were to design this study again?
- What might be the significance of this study to others outside the specific field?
- What are the implications/real life applications to this research?
- Why was this research important? What did you learn?
- Why did you choose to use a quantitative (or qualitative) method in your research? Also discuss your design choice. What were the advantages and disadvantages of these choices?
- What statistics did you use, and why?
- What are the ethical issues involved with this research?
- How can you find others who share your research interests?

Complete Worksheet #2 to develop specific answers to these common questions. Also, use Worksheet #2 to list each committee member who will be at your defense, and try to anticipate the kinds of questions they will ask. Think about their past behavior during meetings with you, comments they raised during the revision process, what they have asked during other student's dissertation defenses, and their area of expertise. For example, one of my committee members had a reputation of asking EVERYONE questions about statistics. Another committee member typically asked how the project findings might relate to his own area of research, so it was important to be familiar with this committee member's research before the defense.

Not so Common Questions

In addition to the specific questions about your dissertation, there will likely be broader questions about the field and research methodology. Try to step back a bit from the myopic focus of your dissertation. Get a broader perspective (easier said than done when all you have been living and breathing is your dissertation!) This, of course, requires some mental flexibility and a more in-depth knowledge about research and your educational field in general.

Despite all of your preparation, there will likely be a few questions you never even considered and catch you by surprise. That is okay—you can't plan for everything. When faced with these surprises, sometimes the committee is looking to see how you respond under pressure, so this is your chance to do so professionally. Believe me, this is good practice for other work in the academic world, for you will often be faced by questions where there are no easy answers (e.g., when you are presenting at a national research conference and there is a tough question from an expert in the room, or when you are teaching a graduate class for the first time and there is a student who challenges you directly).

How to respond? Take a deep breath. Take a moment to think (or a take a drink of water to stall). Be respectful about the question ("That's an interesting question" or "That is a very good point.") Ask for clarification, if needed. Answer to the best of your knowledge. This is your chance to present a viewpoint and defend it with the full range of your professional knowledge. And if you don't know something, as indicated before, be honest. It is appropriate to say you do not know something, state that you will need to research that idea/concept further and send a reply to the committee once you have done so.

Avoid Defensiveness

Although the oral defense is designed for you to demonstrate your scholarly skills and abilities at the doctoral level, the setting is not the proper place to get defensive. In fact, getting defensive may be a showstopper. The committee will very likely want you to make some changes and revisions to your dissertation that will result from either reviewing the dissertation prior to the defense or from your presentation during the oral defense.

Your demeanor should be one of appreciation for the feedback and thankfulness to the committee for their careful reading of your research and their careful listening as your story about the dissertation unfolded. In most cases, the committee will request that the changes be worked out between you and the chair.

It is OK to say: I do not know the answer, but I can get back to you on that issue..

A tool that might help you to keep track of things and to present to your chair along with your revised document is a simple change matrix. A change matrix will usually include changes needed and the associated page numbers along with the changes and revisions you made with associated page numbers. Then, when your chair is satisfied that you have properly addressed the changes, all will be ready to sign the dissertation signature page (that you may want to have framed).

Oral Defense FAQs

Here are some FAQs that may help you to relax and to not fret about the oral defense

Q. Who sets the agenda for the oral defense?

A. The agenda is usually set by the chair in collaboration with you. A typical format follows:

- Introductions and Purpose—Chair
- Oral presentation or PP Presentation—Student (about thirty minutes)
- Q & A—Committee *and Chair* (about thirty to forty minutes)
- Committee discussion without the student (about ten to fifteen minutes)
- Feedback with the *student*—All
- Next steps—*Chair*

So, the oral defense takes about 90 to 105 minutes. In some instances, the defense particularly in a meeting room with a large committee present may go as long as two hours.

Q. What about conference calls?

A. There are a number of free conference call services that are available. The student will usually research the services available and send the dial in numbers and the access codes to the committee a few days before the oral defense.

Q. When will I know the results?

A. In either the in person setting or the conference call setting, after the committee discusses the oral defense, the chair will announce that you passed the oral defense and address you as Doctor.

Q. Does not passing the oral defense occur?

A. There are some infrequent instances of the student failing the oral defense. Not passing the oral defense may be attributed to factors like not being familiar with quantitative as well as qualitative study methods and their associated research designs;

lack of demonstrated competence in regard to answering some detailed questions about the statistics, such as, "Why did you select a certain level of significance?" or "How did you control for Type I and Type II errors?"; and faking answers to questions that you do not know the answer of. If you cannot answer a question, say something like "I do not know the answer to your question, but I will find out and follow up with you."

Q What happens next?

A. After the oral defense and all the requested changes are made and the signature page completed, a typical procedure is to submit the study to the Dean's office for filing. The institution will usually send the dissertation to an archive or database such as ProQuest. In many instances, the oral defense will take place as many as six to ten months before graduation. You can request a letter or transcript documenting that you have completed all the requirements for the doctoral degree. This letter will serve the purpose of qualifying for promotion or pay increase.

It is a good idea to have a number of your dissertations hardbound. The committee really appreciates receiving an autographed copy of your wonderful document that has occupied your life 24/7 for several months. Oh, and reserve a special copy for your mom and dad if you are lucky enough to still have them around. What a thrill it will be for your parents to proclaim to their friends "My daughter or son is a Doctor." Whether still living or not, many students dedicate the dissertation to their parents as an acknowledgement of how they helped you during childhood or adulthood to develop the passion and desire to complete the rigorous doctoral journey.

After your defense and dissertation revisions, it will be time to prepare for graduation. Order your academic regalia, and invite your loved ones to the ceremony. What a thrill it is to have your name announced as you cross the stage to be hooded by your chair or a designated representative of the graduate school.

Now you can go forth as a member of the doctoral community. But do not wait too long to publish the results of your dissertation as an article or submit the results for a presentation at a state or national professional conference. Many new doctors do that first publication as coauthors or copresenters with their chair or a committee member.

Broader Perspective:
What Have You Gained from This Experience?

As you prepare for and complete the oral defense process, it is easy to be caught up in the minute details of your dissertation and the technical aspects of your PowerPoint® presentation. But this is also the time that you may want to think about the larger accomplishment of completing your doctorate. Though you should keep your preparation and discussion focused on the scholarly and research aspects of your dissertation, you may be asked a question or two about your professional development as a person. And even if you aren't asked directly, it would be great to walk into (and out of) your defense with a strong sense of professional identity and confidence. Consider the following:

Ahas and Epiphanies

Throughout the doctoral journey, you have no doubt had some *ahas* as well as epiphanies. Record them for future reference or for sharing with others who are in various stages of their doctoral journey. As a new doctor, others would appreciate your words of encouragement to help them achieve success in the program. You may even be asked about this during your defense.

Personal Mission

Along the way in the doctoral journey, you have studied may have even evaluated mission and vision statements posted by various types of organizations, businesses, schools, and industries. As you know, these statements talk about the nature of the organization, serving employees and customers and, the core values of the organization.

So do you have a personal mission statement? If so, great; if not, then it would be a good scholarly activity to write a personal mission statement. Personal mission statements are usually short and to the point, about one or two sentences. A personal mission statement may also be an important talking point for you during the oral defense, if you are asked directly.

Finding Your Voice

Let's visit finding your voice for a few minutes. Take a look at your chapter 5, with all those wonderful Conclusions and Recommendations. Ask yourself, "Is there something else, or is there something I missed?" What a great question, with an answer that is all about you and your hours and hours of drafting, writing, and rewriting. The answer is finding your voice, but what does that mean? During political campaigns, hearing candidates proclaim that they found their voice is pretty common. What they are referring to is the ups and downs, ins and outs, best of times, and worst of times they experienced as candidates for public office. They drew some conclusions based on looking at political polls, listening to their advisors and consultants, dealing with the press, and drawing some conclusions based on those experiences. In other words, the candidates who proclaim that they found their voice develop a good deal of expertise in regard to figuring out the layout of the political landscape and then delivering messages with competence that made sense to prospective voters.

Similarly, you have now found your doctoral level voice. Think about your doctoral journey, about working with your chair and committee, and about the sacrifices you and your family and friends made to help you through the best of times and the worst of times. Think about the total experiences of the doctoral journey—the content courses online or on ground, residency courses, internship, graduate or research assistant experiences, the research tools, and the long hours at the library and in front of the computer helped you develop that confidence and expertise to speak with authority about your topic. Think about all of the amazing skills and content you have learned through your dissertation process. Then during the oral defense, if asked a question about how you have developed as a professional and what you are going to do after the degree, you can use your doctoral level voice to let your knowledge and expertise shine and come through loud and clear. While your first inclination might be to answer the postdoc question with something like "I will sleep for a week after the degree," save that activity or inactivity for later.

Finding and demonstrating your voice is not a sign of arrogance; it is a validation that you have the knowledge, competence, and skills and abilities to join the doctoral community as a new breed of twenty-first-century scholar and lifelong learner. Your voice will also be a part of your continued research efforts as you publish; present at, or participate in, state, regional, and national conferences; and add to the body of knowledge in your chosen professional discipline.

Closing Comment

All in all, the oral defense and the graduation ceremonies are wonderful celebrations of success—for you and your family; your dissertation chair and the committee members; the university that will have produced another doctoral graduate; the profession; and the students, colleagues, and customers that you serve.

Congratulations! You did it, you earned it, and you deserve to be addressed as DOCTOR!

Worksheet 8.1: Practicing and Improving Your Dissertation Presentation

The key to a smooth presentation is practice, practice, and more practice. Your dissertation chair may ask you to do a *dress rehearsal*, or you can ask if you should practice with him or her. Otherwise, ask trusted friends and colleagues to be your *committee* so that you can practice your presentation and rehearse fielding tough questions. Use this worksheet to help you get feedback on your presentation and revise accordingly. Also, keep track of the questions that your audience members ask; they just might be the same questions that your committee asks you during your defense.

Practice Audience Member	Feedback/Suggestions for Presentation	Questions during Q & A
Name:		
Name:		
Name:		

Worksheet 8.2: Commonly Asked Questions during Dissertation Defense

Consider the following common questions and areas of discussion in a dissertation defense. Write notes to help you prepare to successfully address these questions as they relate to your research.

What is your next step with this research? Discuss future research studies.

What is the biggest limitation or weakness in your dissertation?

What would you do differently, if you were to design this study again?

What might the significance of this study be to others outside the specific field?

What are the implications/real life applications to this research?

Why was this research important? What did you learn?

Why did you choose to use a quantitative (or qualitative) method in your research? Also discuss your design choice. What were the advantages and disadvantages of these choices?

What statistics did you use, and why?

What are the ethical issues involved with this research?

How can you find others who share your research interests?

Other questions:

List each committee member who will be in attendance at the defense. What questions are they likely to ask? Consider their previous behavior during meetings/defenses, involvement with your dissertation, and area of expertise (e.g., statistics, methodology, questions about participant population, ethical issues.) Write down your answers.

Faculty member	Questions they may ask	My answers
Chair:		
Committee member:		
Committee member:		
Committee member:		
Outside reviewer:		
Other:		

Chapter 10

Your Life, After the Dissertation

Tiffany L. Tibbs, PhD

Introduction

"Congratulations! You passed your defense—You are now officially Dr. Tibbs!"

This was the moment I had anticipated, and thought would never come. A mixture of joy, relief, and exhaustion rushed over me. I was done! I couldn't believe it. After shaking hands with everyone and talking jovially with the colleagues who had attended my defense, I gathered my things and walked slowly out of the building in a daze. Though elated, it felt so strange to be done with such a big part of my life. My dissertation had been the focus of my life/time/energy for so long, I remember asking myself, "Now what?" Indeed, what is life like after the dissertation?

The good news is that you actually have a life again. Your life after the dissertation certainly consists of more free time and a lot less on your mind. You should be proud of your success and accomplishment. Take some time to celebrate and relax—you earned it! Reconnect with friends and family. Do things you have postponed because of the dissertation. Revisit your life facet charts from chapter 1 and add or change them to reflect your new status. Thank your dissertation chair and committee members for their service. Participate in your graduation ceremony to mark this special time of life.

But after plenty of celebration and relaxation, it is time to consider how you are actually going to apply all the knowledge and skills you gained from your dissertation. At first, you may think that you never want to read or talk about your dissertation project again! Or you may feel a little lost or letdown, now that the intense focus on your dissertation is done. You may not know the next steps to take. How exactly are you going to use your dissertation experience and expertise?

In some ways, having a fulfilling life *after* the dissertation *begins* much, much earlier in time. It begins when you strategically select a dissertation topic based on your intellectual interests and the doors that topic could open in the future.

Think back to why you wanted to obtain your doctorate in the first place. What goals were you striving for? How did you envision this would change your life? Has that changed over time? What job opportunities become available, now that you have completed your dissertation? Certainly, an advanced degree is a personal milestone, an accomplishment that holds meaning and value in and of itself. But it is also an important stepping-stone, whether that leads to a promotion in your current job or a completely different career.

Turns out, you begin another journey, after your dissertation is complete. But fortunately, you are a wiser traveler this time around, and that is evidenced by the skills you have (not to mention the degree behind your name!) Whether you believe it or feel like it, you are indeed an expert in your field. And your dissertation is not just a book to put on a shelf. The process gave you a chance to learn valuable skills in research, critical thinking, and writing, as well as the diplomatic skills that are necessary to work with a committee. This chapter will help you apply many of those things to your *real life* or *your life, after the dissertation.*

Your Life: What Will You Do Next?

Before we get started with the specifics about how to share your knowledge and further your career, I want to take a moment to discuss a common reaction that people experience in life after the dissertation. Few people talk about it openly in the academic community, and I certainly wasn't prepared for it. I expected to be really excited once my dissertation was finished. But instead, I think I ended up with the postdissertation blues.

After your dissertation is complete, everyone expects that you will be ecstatic ("Doesn't it feel great to be done?" they ask with anticipation) and that you will have a clear plan about your life ("What will you do next?"). Maybe you do feel wonderful, and you have a job lined up immediately after your luxurious vacation. If so, congratulations! Even still, don't be surprised if you don't exactly feel great, or if you don't yet know what you are going to do next, or you can't even think straight after your dissertation! Many people report having this experience after their dissertation, which some have termed *postdissertation stress disorder,* or PDSD. Others have compared it to postpartum depression, calling it *postdissertation depression.* While these are not officially clinical diagnoses, it helps to consider what people have described.

Your specific reaction to the conclusion of your dissertation may differ, but many people have reported something like this following their dissertation . . . You may feel burned out and exhausted, from the chronic stress that you faced during the process. You might feel letdown, like the experience of defending your dissertation was anticlimactic ("Really, that's it? After all that work?") You may not feel comfortable calling yourself a *Dr.* or may fear that you didn't fully deserve your degree. You may feel lost and without the demands and structure of the dissertation, not know exactly what to do with your time and energy. You may feel depressed or anxious and have trouble adjusting to your new normal. Or you may avoid taking the steps needed to publish your dissertation work or further your career.

I am telling you all of this, not to depress you, but rather so that you are not surprised if this does happen to you. It helps to know that this is actually quite common and normal. The specific way you feel (exhausted vs. lost) and degree of distress may vary from person to person. However, if you are prepared that this could happen, it won't be as concerning and surprising. With rest, relaxation, resuming routines, and talking with others, you will start to feel better. You get your energy back; you will start to find your direction. Of course, if you are concerned about your distress or how it is impacting your work or social life, then certainly seek professional help to get you back on track to having a fulfilling life after your dissertation.

The rest of this chapter is designed to show you how to move forward in your life in meaningful ways, using your dissertation experience. Use the tips and worksheets as you move out of your postdissertation stress or depression or exhaustion, or to further capitalize on your postdissertation euphoria (if you are so lucky!).

Sharing Your Knowledge in Publications, Presentations, and Discussions

You have become an expert in your field of study, and that begins a legacy for your professional life. Be ready to share your knowledge; it is good for the field and good for you professionally. Read this section and complete Worksheet 10.1 to help you make concrete plans to share your dissertation with the world.

Share Your Dissertation Professionally through Publications and Presentations

A top priority after finishing your dissertation is to share your knowledge with the professional community. *One of the most important things you can do professionally is to publish your dissertation findings in a relevant professional journal.* This helps you tremendously, as it demonstrates your expertise in this area with a first-authored paper on your curriculum vitae. Publishing your dissertation will make you a more attractive job candidate; shows research productivity, which is helpful for promotion; and lays the groundwork for getting other research started and funded.

One word of wisdom: don't linger too long before publishing your dissertation. Though you may personally be tired of reading, thinking, and writing about topic, it is important to share that work with the world while the material is fresh in your mind. All that hard work (from you, from participants, and from others) deserves to be shared, and this should be reflected in a publication. Waiting will only make it harder and less likely that you will actually get it published.

Adapting your dissertation to a journal requires some homework. Figure out which journals are appropriate and well respected in your research area. For example, which journals did you often cite in your own literature review? Streamlining the text and distilling the results into the most relevant points can be challenging. It is no small task to take one hundred plus pages of dissertation down to ten pages for a journal article. Make sure you know the journal's focus, word limit, and formatting guidelines. Pick the main outcomes you want to report in your first publication, and figure out what secondary issues or additional analyses could be saved for another publication. Dissertations are typically rich in data, so you may be able to get several publications out of it.

Faculty members have knowledge about what text to cut, what to focus on, and which journals are most likely to publish your particular research. Thus, include other coauthors in the process (your chair, colleagues who collaborated), and use their guidance and expertise from the start. Discuss the order of authorship sooner rather than later. Typically, the dissertation student is the first author. Determine writing/editing expectations for team members, and establish a timeline. Expect that there could be rejections or revisions required from journal editors; it is just part of the process. Fortunately, your dissertation process has helped you to become comfortable and familiar with revisions, right?

Another useful way to share your dissertation findings and establish professional connections is to present at research conferences. Ask your chair or committee members about key professional conferences to attend to present your work as a poster or a paper. Faculty members often have great suggestions about how to do this effectively. Presenting a poster or conference presentation requires preparation. For example, you will need to determine the conference standards and format for presentations, the most effective visual way to present data, who your audience will be, and what questions to anticipate. Again, include key coauthors in this process and list them appropriately. Conferences can be excellent places to network with other professionals regarding research opportunities and jobs.

Share Your Dissertation with Interested Groups

You may also want to share the results of your dissertation with groups outside the research arena. *Presenting your dissertation research to an interested local group may provide a useful service for them and connect you with people are good professional contacts.* For example, I did research on the psychological aspects of breast cancer, and I presented my results to a support group for breast cancer patients and providers. This information was timely and helpful for the patients, and I was able to talk with a number of people (patients and physicians alike) who were interested in future research and professional opportunities. You also may want to share your dissertation results, in publication form or via presentation, to the sponsoring organization or recruitment sites that helped you with data collection. For example, if you partnered with a school district to collect data, you may want to present at a district meeting about the results, and help them use what you learned to improve an organization or process.

Share Your Dissertation in Conversations and Job Interviews

Be prepared to share your dissertation in a variety of conversational and interview situations. One skill to cultivate is the ability to talk about your dissertation in a real-world way with individuals who may not be in the academic field but are interested in the topic. Since you are more used to academic discussions, this is a skill that may take some practicing with family members and friends. Focus on the broad topic area and the practical findings and implications from your research. Have a one-minute *elevator pitch* that you could use to succinctly describe your research in a practical way for casual conversations. You never know when a discussion might lead to more discussion, a job opportunity, or a future research partner. Also be prepared to talk for a more extended time during a job interview and tailor the discussion of your dissertation to the audience (e.g., use more applied, practical concepts for a staff member or a person outside of the academia; use more academic, research terminologies for university settings).

Similarly, *be prepared to do a formal job talk, using the results of your dissertation research.* Many academic jobs expect that job candidates will present their topic during a departmental colloquium or a research meeting. Ask your dissertation chair for feedback about your defense performance and how you can adapt that presentation for job talks. Confirm with potential employers what type of job talk will be expected, based on the norms of that department. Tailor your job talk so that it is relevant to the audience and so that it is clear how your research will help a specific department or organization. Practice this presentation so that you are able to deliver it smoothly and field difficult questions; fortunately, this is a time when all of your dissertation defense skills will come in handy!

Continue to Seek Knowledge from Your Chair and Faculty Members

Your dissertation chair and committee members have a wealth of collective knowledge, not just about academic topics, but also about the nuances and process of joining the academic professional ranks. They can continue to be helpful to you in your life after the dissertation is complete, which is yet another reason why it is important to build and maintain good relationships with them.

As mentioned above, it is expected that you would consult with your chair (and other trusted faculty members) about publications, conferences, and job talks. But there are also a number of other ways they can help you develop as a professional. There is a lot of informal acculturation that goes on at universities that may be missing from online programs. Thus, it may be particularly important for students of online universities to directly consult with their chair, faculty members, as well as their colleagues from the program about these career development issues.

- *Ask your chair and committee members about how to effectively search for postdoctoral positions and job opportunities as you get closer to finishing your dissertation.* They can direct you to publications, online listings, and professional groups, depending on your area of research and the type of job you desire. In addition, they might connect you to key people to contact directly about jobs; word of mouth, though old-fashioned, can still be an effective way to find out about positions. You will likely need to start getting applications and inquiries started before you finish your dissertation. Find out how and when jobs typically are posted and filled. Start early!

- *Learn more about how to interview and negotiate for specific jobs.* Faculty members likely have a good sense about what questions to ask, what key resources to request as part of a job offer, what salary and benefits are appropriate, what pitfalls to avoid, and what not to ask for based on the norms of the academic world.

- *Ask for recommendation letters from your dissertation chair when you are applying for jobs.* In the future, you may also need recommendation letters when you are up for a promotion as well. Give them enough notice to complete this process well. Also discuss what will help to facilitate this process. For example, would it be helpful for them to have your updated curriculum vitae? Job description for the position? A document from you about your strengths and accomplishments or why you would be excellent for this position? These items may help to construct a letter that is personalized and compelling.

- *Determine what other publications or grant projects you could work on in the future.* Faculty members often know about a range of projects and publications that are available. They may not have the time to do it themselves, but they might be thrilled to see a junior faculty member lead the project. Grant writing is a complicated skill, so it would be helpful to partner with an accomplished grant-writing faculty member.

- *Find out their recommendations about best practices for mentoring students;* believe it or not, you will likely assume responsibilities of mentoring other students and colleagues as you advance in your career.

- *Stay in touch with key faculty members through attendance at conferences and through e-mail.* Periodically update them about your relevant professional accomplishments and ask if there are other job opportunities or colleagues that might be good connections for you. Your chair and committee members will likely continue to move up the academic ranks and to different universities, thus extending your network in a positive way.

Applying Your Knowledge and Skills to Further Your Career

Now that you have completed your degree, *consider how your job opportunities have expanded, whether that is advancing in your current position, getting promoted within an organization, or obtaining a new job.* This section highlights all of the different skills that you have obtained from working on your dissertation and how these can be applied to different work settings. This section, along with Worksheet 10.2, will help you consider how your dissertation experience can help you continue to develop professionally.

Skills Gained in the Process of Completing Your Dissertation

Besides the *content* area of expertise you gained from your dissertation, you also gained a lot of skills during the *process*. These skills will help you find and perform in a variety of different jobs. Consider how completing the dissertation helped you with

- critical thinking skills
- thoroughly researching a topic through an extensive literature review
- designing and conducting a study, with knowledge regarding study methods and designs
- analyzing data and implementing statistical knowledge
- writing and revision skills
- presentation skills during the proposal defense and dissertation defense
- working ethically with study participants
- working collaboratively with your chair and committee members
- envisioning a project and seeing it through from beginning to end
- the list goes on and on . . .

Take some time to think about how personally and professionally you have changed and improved as a result of completing your dissertation.

Applying Your Skills to Different Jobs

The skills you learned from successfully working on your dissertation can be applied to a variety of areas in your professional life. The good news is that you have now sharpened a wide range of skills that can be effectively tailored to make you more professionally marketable. Different jobs in different settings may value one type of skill more than another (e.g., teaching vs. research, scholarly publications vs. service or administrative responsibilities). *Find out the skills and tasks that are valued in particular settings, then apply your knowledge to be effective in those areas.*

Consider how the skills and knowledge from your dissertation experience helped you to effectively do the following:

- *Identify a problem that needs investigation and develop a project to help find solutions.* This could apply in the workplace (e.g., school district, health care organization) or in the academic world, as you further develop your area of research and design new studies. Your dissertation process taught you to put in the necessary time at the beginning of a major project to make sure you have a solid foundation (problem, purpose, research questions) rather than just haphazardly getting something done. Thoughtful consideration initially makes for a smoother process overall. It also taught you how to critically analyze the results and develop recommendations for solutions to the problem.

- *Conduct new research and publish scholarly work, which are very important in academic life.* Depending on the university and job you select, publications can be a major factor in promotions and success in departments and universities. Your dissertation publication and subsequent articles from your research will set you on the right track. Your experience writing, revising, and responding to (committee) reviews will serve you well as you submit to journals. Your experience presenting at your dissertation defense will help you present effectively at professional conferences and meetings.

- *Teach undergraduate and graduate students, which can be a fulfilling part of your professional life.* Depending on the institution, teaching can be one of the key components of your job. You can incorporate the body of knowledge you acquired from your dissertation into lectures, and you will likely be a better reviewer of student writing and papers as a result of your extensive dissertation writing and revision process. You can also apply what worked well and what was difficult about your own experience when you get the opportunity to mentor students in research projects.

- *Obtain grant funding, which may also be a valued component of your job.* In fact, the grant-writing process is similar to the dissertation process in many ways. You need to make a compelling argument about why your research is relevant and important, design a thoughtful and feasible project, work with a range of team members to strengthen the application, be prepared to respond to critical reviews, revise and resubmit multiple times before achieving funding. Grant writing uses a number of other skills and guidelines that can make things challenging, so it is best to work with a successful grant writer/ senior faculty member to learn the tricks of the trade. You need to select funding sources and projects carefully, not to mention have a publication record, to be successful in this arena.

- *Find experienced mentors and team members, in your workplace or a research setting.* Seeking a mentor in the workplace can help you successfully negotiate a new environment and complete key projects. Don't be afraid to ask questions or acknowledge your lack of experience in an area. It will save time to talk with and learn from someone who has already been successful or completed similar tasks initially. Select someone who is experienced and successful in an area you would like to explore professionally. Just as you investigated a dissertation chair, do your homework about who could help you learn something valuable. What kind of expertise does this person have? Are they available and willing to mentor a junior employee? Do you get along well professionally? Determine the parameters of the relationship, how often you will meet or communicate, and what the expectations will be for the relationship.

- *Assemble a diverse team to make research projects, service assignments, or administrative processes better.* Just as you carefully considered who should be on your dissertation committee, be thoughtful about whom you choose to work with on a major project. Personality and work style, strengths and liabilities are all important factors to consider. Use your experience working with your chair and committee members to help you successfully run projects, collaborate with others, and lead teams.

- *Strive for open communication with team members, productive meetings, and clearly defined goals and responsibilities.* These practices will make it more likely that you will be successful in any project. These are skills you honed during your dissertation project and with your committee. They will serve you well whether you are writing a research grant, establishing a new project, or taking a new position in your company.

Congratulations! And best wishes on your new journey in your life after the dissertation.

Worksheet 10.1: Sharing Your Dissertation in Publications, Presentations, and Discussions

PUBLICATIONS:

What professional journals would be a good fit for your dissertation publication?

What are the main points that you want to communicate in a first publication from your dissertation?

Who will be the coauthors? Order of authors? Responsibilities?

What is your target deadline for submitting your adapted dissertation work to a journal?

What are possible secondary papers that could come from your dissertation or data?

Presentations:

What professional conferences would be a good fit for a research poster or presentation from your dissertation?

List the deadlines for application submissions for conferences of interest.

What other audiences or groups would benefit from hearing the results of your dissertation (local professional group, recruitment sites, etc.)?

Discussions

Write a one-minute *elevator pitch* that succinctly describes your dissertation in an accessible way.

What are the key points you would discuss in a conversation or interview about your dissertation findings, using practical language for a person who is not in the academic field?

What are the key points you would discuss for someone who is in your academic field of expertise?

Worksheet 10.2: Using Your Dissertation Experience and Key Contacts to Further Your Career

Think back to what motivated you to become an expert in this field. What you do want to do with your expertise/degree? What kinds of job opportunities now become possible with your advanced degree?

When applying for jobs or promotions, in addition to expertise in your *content* area, what are some of the other skills and strengths that you want to emphasize from successfully completing the dissertation *process*?

List all the formal and informal places to search for job opportunities (publications, social media groups, professional groups).

List all of the people you should contact to let them know you are looking for a job, and what types of jobs would fit your strengths and education.

Who can you ask to write a recommendation letter for your potential job application(s)? What documents/information would help them to write the best letter possible?

Who can you talk to about the job search, interview tips, and negotiation strategies for particular positions? Consider formal and informal sources of information (e.g., your dissertation chair to discuss what salary or research resources to negotiate vs. friends to practice mock interview questions).

What are the key things to ask during job interviews? Or be prepared to answer? (As noted in the previous worksheet, be prepared to discuss your dissertation to academic and nonacademic staff.)

What are the expectations of the potential employer regarding a job talk using your dissertation findings? Length? Focus? Audience?

Find out what professional skills are valued in potential jobs you are seeking (e.g., teaching experience, research experience, publications, grant writing). How much time is devoted to these tasks on the job? How will success be measured on this job for future promotions (e.g., classes taught, funding obtained, scholarly publications)? How does the employer help facilitate success in these areas?

APPENDIX A

Prospectus outline:
What do you want to study and how?

1) What is your research topic or area of study?
_____
_____
_____
_____

2) What type of methods will you use? [*Quantitative/Qualitative/Mixed/Action Research*]
_____
_____
_____
_____

3) What are your research questions? [*no more than four*]
_____
_____
_____
_____

- If you are considering a quantitative study, what is your hypothesis? [*one hypothesis for each research question; provide null and alternate*]
  - _____
  - _____
  - _____
  - _____

4) What is the issue you are attempting to deal with in the study? [*problem*]

_____

_____

_____

_____

5) What is it you are attempting to do in the study? [*purpose*]

_____

_____

_____

6) Why is this study worth doing? [*significance* and *rationale*]

_____

_____

_____

_____

7) What population will you identify for your study?

_____

_____

_____

8) How will you obtain a sample from the above population? [*participants, data source*]

_____

_____

_____

_____

9) How will you gather the data for your study? [interviews, surveys/questionnaires, focus groups, observations, etc.]

_____

_____

_____

_____

10) Explain how each source of data will help answer your question or test your hypothesis [*operationalize each variable being collected; how does it relate to the RQ or the hypothesis*]

_____

_____

_____

_____

11) Research context [*Elementary Education, Online Education, Secondary Education, Organizational Management, Healthcare Legislation, etc.*]

_____

_____

_____

_____

12) What is your relationship to the participants? [*boss, colleague/peer, researcher*]

_____

_____

_____

_____

13) Time frame [*when to gather data*]

_____

_____

_____

_____

APPENDIX B

Concept Paper Outline

Introduction

Statement of the Problem

Purpose of the Study

Research Questions
    Hypotheses [*Quantitative/Mixed studies only*]

Definition of Key Terms

Brief Review of the Literature
    Theme/Subtopic 1 [*Repeat, as needed . . .*]

Research Method

Operational Definition of Variables [*Quantitative/Mixed studies only*] *or* Defining the Construct as a Variable [*Qualitative studies only*]

Measurement

Summary

References

From the authors of Dissertation and Research Success comes an exciting new place for you to go for help with your dissertation and research needs. Introducing…………....................……

Dissertation and Research Assist

Spend time with a dissertation/research **coach*** as needed to assist in completing your masters/doctoral level work, getting materials ready for publication, developing research ideas, and creating a team of colleagues as you move forward in your research endeavors.

We offer the following assistance:

24/7	Email Help Line
24/7	Website references and helpful materials
24/7	Website discussion boards, blogs, and self –paced tutorials
24/7	Small group sessions/workspace
By Appt:	Personal 1 on 1 teleconferences
Office Hours	Regularly scheduled days/times

More to come:

Expansion of Web related references, tools, and support.

Live (face-to-face small group conference time (weekend format).

Contact Information:

Email:	dissertationandresearchassist@gmail.com
Website:	www.dissertationandresearchassist.com

- **NOTE: All coaches are highly experienced research and doctoral level faculty. All have professional credentials and are published authors in their field.**